DAIL

YOUR IMAGE

Reflecting the Character of Christ

REBECCA BARLOW JORDAN

BARBOUR
PUBLISHING

Published by Barbour Publishing, Inc., P.O. Box 719, Uhrichsville, Ohio 44683, www.barbourbooks.com

Our mission is to publish and distribute inspirational products offering exceptional value and biblical encouragement to the masses.

Member of the
Evangelical Christian
Publishers Association

Printed in the United States of America.
5 4 3 2 1

Dedication

To my husband, Larry,
who reflects the character of Christ
more than anyone I know.

Special Thanks

I could not write about the character of Christ without thanking those who reflect Him so beautifully.

Thanks to the entire staff of Barbour Publishing, including the sales and marketing team, for believing in my manuscript, for their helpfulness and dedication, and for helping to visualize the final product; to Debbie Peterson, who edited the manuscript; to designer Robyn Martins, who gave this book its beautiful cover; to typesetters Gladys Dunlap and Sharon Dean; and especially to my editor, Kelly Williams, for believing in me, for her warm enthusiasm and helpful, encouraging spirit, and for her patience and expertise in answering all of my questions.

Thanks to my husband, Larry, for his constant support and encouragement to seek the Father's heart, for luring me out of bed each morning with hot coffee on the bedside table, and for his love, prayers, and understanding throughout the process of every book I write. He is my inspiration!

Thanks to others who prayed me through the writing of this book: family members, friends, church members, my Bible study class, and again, my faithful prayer support team of women: Ruth, Priscilla, Mary, Sharon, and Kim.

Thanks to my new agent, Steve Laube, who stepped in to help negotiate and seal the contract.

Most of all, thanks to my precious Lord Jesus Christ, for mirroring the Father so beautifully, for giving me the privilege of writing about Him, for loving me so unconditionally—and for patiently working on my character so that one day I might truly reflect His.

Introduction

We cannot by sheer willpower attain Christlikeness. No matter how determined, how dedicated, or how disciplined we are, we cannot embody all of Christ's character overnight. However, the moment we reach out in faith to Him, we begin the process of reflecting the character of Christ. A new spirit is born in us immediately, but God knows our frame. We are changed from the inside out. He uses every means possible to make us His reflectors. Sometimes it is the trying of our faith that results in qualities like patience and endurance. Sometimes a crushing blow on the Potter's wheel reshapes our character and helps form the desired product. His powerful Word instructs; His living Spirit corrects; His gentle hand guides. And always His goodness and love can bring change—and the desire to move forward at an even greater speed.

But God knows it takes a lifetime to make us like Himself. He is a patient and loving God. And He never abandons the ones He is shaping.

What can we do to hasten the process? Oh, that God could unzip us and pour all of His grace and kindness and goodness into us in one giant motion—and then zip us back up for an eternity of perfection. But that's impossible, or is it? In Jesus' death and resurrection, He poured out all of Himself as a supreme sacrifice so that God could then supernaturally clothe us with His perfection and seal us with His Spirit. There's only one problem. We don't understand what all is available to us. Someone convinces us that our new nature is not real, like wearing the "emperor's new clothes," and because our "clothing" is invisible to us and everyone else, we assume the King really didn't dress us royally after all. Maybe we really didn't inherit throne rights. Instead of acting like our King's kids, maybe we start living as paupers again. Or we live on the edge, working furiously, trying so hard to become the persons we already are.

The psalmist chose some decisions that made Christlikeness more of a reality. Study the "I wills" of Psalms and experience the hunger and devotion of the human soul for more of God. Was the psalmist perfect in his performance? No, the writer of most of Psalms—David—was as human a man as you will find anywhere. Yet he was dubbed "a man after God's own heart." Why? Because he pursued God with all his heart. Because he understood who God was. And because God had a purpose for David's life.

Paul, too, admitted the battle he fought between two natures: his own desire for Christlikeness and the tendency to live for himself. Yet he pursued God with all his heart. To reflect Christ's image was his all-consuming, lifelong passion: "To me, to live is Christ." He not only understood who Christ was; he understood who he was in Christ. He *chose* to reflect the One he loved.

We, too, face a choice. To reflect Christ, to live in His image—or to reflect the images of others around us. God's power is available. He created us in His own image. He simply wants our trust, our obedience, and our love. He may move us past our comfort zones to accomplish His purpose, to make us more like Him. The process may even be quite painful and leave scars.

It was impossible for me to focus on the attributes of God for so long without developing a hunger to know Him even more deeply and a constant desire to reflect the character of Christ in my life. In my book *Daily in Your Presence: Intimate Conversations with a Loving Father*, I shared 366 names and attributes of the Triune God. I hope you discovered in that devotional the very precious and faithful nature of an intimate Father, a personal Christ, and a powerful Holy Spirit—and that you fell head over heels in love with the One who loves you so much.

In this new book, *Daily in Your Image*, I pray you will be challenged to let the very character of Christ saturate your heart and that you will join me in making your all-consuming desire not only to know Him and to love Him—but to be like Jesus. I urge you to use this devotional guide often—not just once a day—but for a lifetime, to remind you of the 366 ways you can reflect the character of Christ.

Daily, Christ is working, conforming us to His image. Right now, we can see only a partial reflection; but one day, when we stand with Jesus, we will look into that mirror and see a perfect reflection of the One we pursued with all our hearts—the One who loves us with all of His heart. I'm looking forward to that moment of seeing Jesus face-to-face. I promise you—no, *He* promises you—it will all be worthwhile then. He is faithful!

REBECCA

*Now we see but a poor reflection as in a mirror;
then we shall see face to face. Now I know in part;
then I shall know fully, even as I am fully known.*

1 CORINTHIANS 13:12

DECISIVENESS

*"Choose for yourselves this day whom you will serve. . . .
But as for me and my household, we will serve the LORD."*

JOSHUA 24:15

FROM THE FATHER'S HEART

My child, when you learn to choose wisely for yourself the attitudes, actions, and directions you want for your life, you are developing decisiveness. It is recognizing that with My help you can choose confidently what is right, what is helpful, what is best, and what will honor Me the most. Listen for My voice. I will help you with every decision you make.

FROM A SEEKING HEART

Father, there are times when even the most minute decisions try to paralyze me. I long to hear Your definitive voice saying, "Walk here. Turn here." Teach me Your values; let my thoughts and decisions reflect the mind of Christ. I want to serve You, Lord. Today I take my stand with You. My heart's desire is to honor You every day of my life.

SIMPLE TRUTH

When it comes to serving God, indecisiveness is still a decision.

ABANDONMENT

*"Anyone who does not take his cross and follow me
is not worthy of me."*

MATTHEW 10:38

FROM THE FATHER'S HEART

My child, as you become willing to follow Me at all costs,
turning your back on anything else that has previously held
you in its grip, you are learning abandonment. While doing
so may seem difficult, My rewards pay great dividends.
When you choose to surrender your own self-will, interests,
and desires, I will exchange them for a brand-new heart and
life that is pleasing to Me.

FROM A SEEKING HEART

Lord, not a day passes without the struggle for abandonment. I want more than anything for You to rule and self to
die. Take my dreams, my plans, and my life. Lord, remove
every useless piece of furniture. Empty every room of my
heart if necessary. Whatever it takes, Lord, I long to be
filled up with You. I abandon myself to You.

SIMPLE TRUTH

When Jesus issues His call, we must surrender our all.

ADMINISTRATION

And God said, "I will be with you."

EXODUS 3:12

FROM THE FATHER'S HEART

My child, I will help you carry out My wishes in the most effective way possible. I will teach you administration. Don't be discouraged. You cannot do My work alone. But with My help, you can direct others to find purposeful avenues for their creativity while you try to make a difference in My world.

FROM A SEEKING HEART

Father, I want neither to cling selfishly to the pride of self-sufficiency nor to cower from the responsibility of leadership. Any good I can do is because of You, and I know You have equipped me for any task, no matter how great or small. Teach me the joy of discipleship. Give me the wisdom to know when to delegate work to others in Your kingdom, so we can all hear Your "Well done."

SIMPLE TRUTH

I would like neither to burn out nor to rust out but to serve out my years with faithfulness to God.

EXCELLENCE

*. . .so that you may approve what is excellent,
and may be pure and blameless for the day of Christ.*

PHILIPPIANS 1:10 RSV

FROM THE FATHER'S HEART

My child, do you desire to give Me all that you are for all
that I am? Then you want excellence. It is not demanding
perfection of yourself or others. That has never been My
will for you. But it is choosing to value what I value and to
love what I love in light of eternity. When you do that, you
will be choosing the more excellent way.

FROM A SEEKING HEART

Father, You deserve the best. Yet my gifts seem so small and
insignificant, and my heart longs to honor You. Forgive my
misguided efforts at perfectionism and my failure to accept
others as they are. Lord, I want more of You, so that everything I do, everything I think about, and everything I am
will reflect You. Today, Lord, I'm choosing excellence.

SIMPLE TRUTH

Only God can turn imperfect perfectionism into excellence.

AMBITION

*Delight yourself in the LORD
and he will give you the desires of your heart.*

PSALM 37:4

FROM THE FATHER'S HEART

My child, the kind of ambition I want for you is the persistent desire to reach your full potential in Me, recognizing that I alone am the Giver of every good and perfect gift. As you place your aspirations in My hands, I will work out the details of your life and develop those abilities and talents that you place at My disposal.

FROM A SEEKING HEART

Lord, in the past I have often reached for the stars instead of for You. No longer will I nurture hidden desires that lead me away from Your presence. No more will I seek after temporary pleasures that leave me dissatisfied and disillusioned. All that You are is all that I ever want to be. You are the real Star of my life! And knowing You is my lifelong ambition.

SIMPLE TRUTH

God wants to bring us to the place where His dreams become our dreams.

SINGLE-MINDEDNESS

*Let us throw off everything that hinders. . .
and let us run with perseverance the race marked out for us.*

HEBREWS 12:1

FROM THE FATHER'S HEART

My child, your willingness to remove all distractions, good or bad, that may hinder My work in your life will help you become single-minded. If you will let Me, I will help you concentrate on what is important and of eternal value. Fix your eyes on Me. I will not only help you run the race well, but I will be there to applaud your victory at the end.

FROM A SEEKING HEART

Lord, I cannot run my life's race with all the baggage I have carried in the past. Today I'm asking You to help me remove these unwanted weights. I can almost hear the cheers from those witnesses that have gone before me. And I want to follow Your example as You single-mindedly carried out the perfect will of Your Father.

SIMPLE TRUTH

Weight lifting increases physical strength, but weight removal is what our spirits need.

BOLDNESS

*And they were all filled with the Holy Spirit
and spoke the word of God with boldness.*

ACTS 4:31 RSV

FROM THE FATHER'S HEART

My child, I long to give you boldness and the confident assurance that I am in control. When you surrender your fears and hesitations to Me, I will empower you with a holy boldness and fill you with My Spirit so that you can speak My words, not your own. No longer will you need to cower behind excuses. My Spirit will free you!

FROM A SEEKING HEART

Father, just when I think fear is under control, I'm tempted to let my knees buckle and my heart shrink. I need Your strength daily, Lord. Today I'm taking my eyes off my weaknesses and my challenging circumstances. Fill me with the fresh fire of Your boldness so that others might see and hear the fruits of Your holy presence. Today I'm declaring my freedom in Christ and the boldness to declare Your truth wherever You lead.

SIMPLE TRUTH

Boldness moves us from comfort to conquest.

ACCOUNTABILITY

*Therefore, I urge you, brothers, in view of God's mercy,
to offer your bodies as living sacrifices, holy and pleasing to God—
this is your spiritual act of worship.*

ROMANS 12:1

FROM THE FATHER'S HEART

My child, I will teach you the importance of accountability as you humble yourself before Me and recognize that your actions, thoughts, and attitudes affect those around you. I will place other godly servants around you who will also help you become responsible and accountable for your own growth and behavior. When you pull away from Me, you grow weak and ineffective. Stay close, My child. Stay close.

FROM A SEEKING HEART

Lord, I feel so alone when I venture out into the deep without You or the support of others. Just as You were accountable to Your Father, I, too, need that accountability with You. Today I'm offering You a living sacrifice and asking Your Spirit to give me a holy check each time I try to head the opposite direction. And today I will enlist at least three other trusted friends to help keep me accountable.

SIMPLE TRUTH

*Even the best solo flyer still depends on the wind
beneath his wings.*

KEENNESS

I pray also that the eyes of your heart
may be enlightened in order that you may know
the hope to which he has called you.

EPHESIANS 1:18

FROM THE FATHER'S HEART

My child, do you want the ability to perceive My leading in your life? Keenness will come as you make My Word top priority in your life and meditate daily on My truths. When you do that, I will open your eyes and give you the direction and understanding you need for the present *and* the future.

FROM A SEEKING HEART

Father, how I need to see with Your eyes and to hear with Your ears—to perceive Your truth in every situation. Only You, Lord, can clearly replace my vision so I can see Your plans for my life through heaven's eyes. Whether it's clear, cloudy, or stormy, Lord, I will choose to view life with keenness.

SIMPLE TRUTH

Nothing makes sense until we view it through
heaven's eyes.

READINESS

They received the word with all readiness of mind,
and searched the scriptures daily.

ACTS 17:11 KJV

FROM THE FATHER'S HEART

My child, I sense your eager pursuit to discover all I have in store for your life. You can choose readiness when you place yourself in a position for My blessing and obey with a learner's spirit, and let Me teach and work through you. Keep My words ever in your thoughts—and you will be prepared for anything.

FROM A SEEKING HEART

Lord Jesus, I can tell the difference when I begin the day hastily and unprepared. Just like Your heart was ready for anything, I, too, want to be prepared. I desire for Your words to be like hidden gold. Daily, I will go digging so I can run after You with all my heart, soul, and mind and "catch" You at work. There, in Your Word and in my heart, You plant nuggets that will help prepare me for every challenge.

SIMPLE TRUTH
Lord, Your command is my wish.

CONGENIALITY

*May the God of steadfastness and encouragement
grant you to live in such harmony with one another,
in accord with Christ Jesus.*

ROMANS 15:5 RSV

FROM THE FATHER'S HEART

My child, as you are willing to accept others in a spirit of love
and peace, you will learn congeniality. If you will let Me, I will
help you temper your thoughts and actions for the unity of all,
so you can open your life to others without fear. I want others to know My love through you. You have so much to give.
Don't be afraid to embrace others with genuine joy!

FROM A SEEKING HEART

Lord, You did not live to please Yourself, but You accepted
others wherever they were. I, too, desire that congenial spirit
that bears with the failings of the weak and yet lives unselfishly as an example of a true believer. Today, Lord, I
choose the kind of spirit that will build up and not tear
down. Let my heart be an open door that says, "Come in!
You're welcome here!"

SIMPLE TRUTH

*Everyone wears an invisible welcome sign that says
"Open" or "Closed."*

ELOQUENCE

The tongue of the righteous is choice silver. . . .
The lips of the righteous feed many.

PROVERBS 10:20–21 RSV

FROM THE FATHER'S HEART

My child, do you desire eloquence? I will give you the ability to inspire, persuade, and motivate others to reach out beyond themselves for the cause of My kingdom. You may feel like you have nothing to offer. But when I have placed My stamp on your life and message, there are no limitations. As you allow Me to develop My gifts within you, I can touch others in extraordinary ways through you.

FROM A SEEKING HEART

Lord, I read about Your simple life; yet Your words fed the souls of multitudes. It was not only what You said but how You said it—with the commanding authority and excellence of heaven. I, too, want to make my words and my life count. In myself, I am not eloquent. But if You will shape the words and the motivation behind them, together we can do great things.

SIMPLE TRUTH

It's not what we speak that matters but Who is speaking through us.

MEEKNESS

Put on then, as God's chosen ones,
holy and beloved, compassion, kindness, lowliness, meekness. . .

COLOSSIANS 3:12 RSV

FROM THE FATHER'S HEART

My child, I love to clothe you with meekness when you release your rights to Me. You are not your own. I chose you and bought you, but I gave you the opportunity to decide for yourself. As I am gentle with you, you can be approachable, valuing the feelings of others rather than constantly demanding your own way. This will not only bring glory to Me but will open the door to others' hearts and create an atmosphere of love so they can listen.

FROM A SEEKING HEART

Lord, I love Your meekness—the quiet strength You demonstrated day after day as You were challenged and stretched. How I value that! Lord, demanding I know the right way instead of giving others the right-of-way will only isolate me from You and others. Today I choose meekness, not weakness.

SIMPLE TRUTH

God is the only One who is right 100 percent of the time.

INTEGRITY

*In my integrity you uphold me
and set me in your presence forever.*

PSALM 41:12

FROM THE FATHER'S HEART

My child, you have integrity when you know you are complete in Me. When you consciously put Me first, you can live in peace, even when others may criticize or discount your actions. It's not so important what others think, but what I think that matters most. Integrity will choose wisely every time.

FROM A SEEKING HEART

Father, only You know the backdoor entrance to my heart. No one but You holds the keys to all the hidden closets. Sweep away every cobweb, and invade every room with Your presence. I cannot choose wisely how to love, how to think, or how to act unless You take over every part of my heart. Only then, Lord, can I act with integrity. Today I accept my completeness in You.

SIMPLE TRUTH

Criticism can drive us to despair or to our knees in prayer.

ACCURACY

*"I open my lips to speak what is right.
My mouth speaks what is true."*

PROVERBS 8:6–7

FROM THE FATHER'S HEART

My child, when your ears, eyes, and heart are tuned to My Spirit so I can speak My thoughts through you, you will develop accuracy. Because you are Mine, you can know My voice and discern it from all others. You no longer need to be deceived by false doctrine. Listen carefully to My voice so that your words will echo Mine.

FROM A SEEKING HEART

Lord, I know that what I put into my heart is what will eventually take root and grow. People are dying for the truth, and I am living so I can tell it. Plant Your words in my mind, in my heart, and in my spirit so that I may accurately be Your voice to others, Lord. Today I choose to listen to Your voice only and to accurately speak only Your words.

SIMPLE TRUTH

To hear God's voice accurately requires listening with our spiritual ears.

WONDER

*As soon as all the people saw Jesus,
they were overwhelmed with wonder.*

MARK 9:15

FROM THE FATHER'S HEART

My child, when you can still see My words and My world with childlike eyes, with innocence and purity, I know you have developed wonder. Take time to observe what I have made. Acknowledge My hand in everything, and let My Word open your eyes to a new sense of amazement. Never lose the wonder of life, and I will transform every ordinary event into an extraordinary miracle.

FROM A SEEKING HEART

Lord, sometimes I exhibit childishness instead of a childlike spirit. Keep alive in me the wonder of a new-fallen snowflake, the joy of a first Christmas, and the enthusiasm of a new believer eager to bask in Your love and grace. When practicality tries to snuff out the miraculous, remind me of the wonder in knowing You. Today I choose to view life with true wonder.

SIMPLE TRUTH

Seeing God's world through a child's eyes makes life wonder-full.

DEDICATION

*Be thou faithful unto death,
and I will give thee a crown of life.*

REVELATION 2:10 KJV

FROM THE FATHER'S HEART

My child, you may be only one person, but with My help, you can make a difference. Faithfully dedicate yourself to the unique task for which I have called you, whether it is binding up the wounded, encouraging the weary, or challenging the prejudices of others. Then leave the results to Me.

FROM A SEEKING HEART

Lord, Your dedication is an inspiration to me. You told us we would do even greater works than You; yet my works seem so small at times. Nevertheless, I dedicate myself to follow Your example in great or small things. I'm asking You to do the work through me so that in the end I can present back to You my crown of life. With all that I am and all that You have given to me, I choose to run my race with sincere dedication.

SIMPLE TRUTH

Dedication may require perspiration.

UNPRETENTIOUSNESS

*Now that you have purified yourselves by obeying the truth
so that you have sincere love for your brothers,
love one another deeply, from the heart.*

1 PETER 1:22

FROM THE FATHER'S HEART

My child, there is no need to mask your true self. A willingness to relate to others with deep sincerity and love means you are demonstrating unpretentiousness. Keep the curtains of your heart open. When you accept yourself as you are—the way I created you—then you can see how deeply I love everyone and want you to accept and love others as they are as well.

FROM A SEEKING HEART

Father, I want my heart to be an open book before You and others—clearly read and easily understood. Protect me from backward glances and foolish chances that destroy my ability to love with purity and openness. Let there be nothing hidden or undisclosed that will hinder my relationships with others. You have told me I am a work in progress. So today, Lord, and every day, I choose unpretentiousness as I relate to others.

SIMPLE TRUTH

"Putting on airs" won't get us anywhere—and usually results in a bag of wind.

EXPECTANCY

My soul, wait thou only upon God;
for my expectation is from him.

PSALM 62:5 KJV

FROM THE FATHER'S HEART

My child, live each day in expectancy—the knowledge that
I hold all things in My hand and that I have a definite plan
for your life. As you wait on Me, I will develop within you
a spirit of victory over the past, contentment for the present,
and excitement for the future.

FROM A SEEKING HEART

Father, "hurry up" often replaces my intention to wait on
You. I'm tempted to grab for instant gratification, seeking to
meet needs myself. Lord, teach me to wait only upon You.
You're the One who created me, and You know exactly what
I need. I'm excited to see Your plans unfold. Lord, You alone
hold my future. Like a bride with expectancy for her groom,
I anticipate loving You more and walking in Your presence
daily. Lord, my expectation truly is in You.

SIMPLE TRUTH

When God holds our future, we can expect the
unexpected.

COMMON SENSE

Understanding is a fountain of life to those who have it.

PROVERBS 16:22

FROM THE FATHER'S HEART

My child, you can exercise common sense by thinking My thoughts in every situation. Common sense means the refusal to act foolishly and the willingness to make decisions based on My wisdom, not your own. Your peers will try to pressure you into following their ways and ideas. But I'm waiting to empower you. Will you let Me today?

FROM A SEEKING HEART

Lord, sometimes I still act impulsively without thinking things through. Your only impulse was to do Your Father's will. Let my very first impression be, "What would Jesus do?" and then release every other impulse but that. Your Word says I have the mind of Christ. Today I will act with confidence, using the common sense You have given me. Through Your Spirit, Lord, draw others to the fountain of living water that bubbles within me.

SIMPLE TRUTH

Actions without thought are like tornadoes without warning.

STAMINA

Endure hardship with us like a good soldier of Christ Jesus.

2 TIMOTHY 2:3

FROM THE FATHER'S HEART

My child, I love to give you stamina when you depend on My timetable rather than your own. Stamina means you can trust in My power to strengthen you in your weakness, comfort you in your affliction, and teach you in your difficulties. As a true soldier, you can work without weariness, knowing I am always with you.

FROM A SEEKING HEART

Lord, even Your own disciples tempted You to shortcut Your heavenly Father's plan; yet You remained strong. Like a soldier in battle and just like You, Jesus, I choose to exercise stamina and endure to the end of my assignment. With You walking beside me, giving me strength and encouragement, I will keep pressing on.

SIMPLE TRUTH

Holding on to Jesus will keep us hanging in the race.

FORESIGHT

"Watch out that you are not deceived."

LUKE 21:8

FROM THE FATHER'S HEART

My child, you can exercise foresight by listening to My warnings rather than the reasoning of others. Everyone has an opinion and will want you to hear it. But when you try to see life from My viewpoint and heed My cautions, you will avoid so many needless deceptions. Listen carefully. I will help you think and act wisely.

FROM A SEEKING HEART

Father, so many claim to know the truth: "Follow me! I know the way!" But without thinking for myself, I've tried their paths, and they only led to dead-end streets. You have made me wiser, Lord. Today—and in the future—with Your help, I will act with foresight. I will approach yellow lights with caution. I will plan well, using the mind of Christ You have given me.

SIMPLE TRUTH

Wise thinking avoids needless sinking.

UNITY

*The body of Christ may be built up until
we all reach unity in the faith and
in the knowledge of the Son of God.*

EPHESIANS 4:12–13

FROM THE FATHER'S HEART

My child, when you line up your thoughts and actions
with My purposes, you are developing unity. As you seek to
know Me intimately, I will not only bring you into a oneness
with Myself, but I will also encourage you to strengthen
others in their daily walk. My body on earth is important
to Me. Let Me use you to bring unity.

FROM A SEEKING HEART

Lord, it's exciting to be a part of the body of Christ here on
earth. Show me my place in that body. Help me use my gifts
in such a way that will build up and edify Your kingdom. I
want a solid, mature faith that is not tossed around by every
strange teaching. I want to be one with You! Today I will
cooperate with You to develop unity.

SIMPLE TRUTH

*A body in which parts cease to function can become an
invalid quickly.*

MODERATION

Let your moderation be known unto all men.

Philippians 4:5 kjv

From the Father's Heart

My child, you will learn moderation when you are willing to let Me restrain any activities, thoughts, or actions that might be harmful to yourself and others. Instead of preferring your own selfish ways, you can choose what will help others and the cause of Christ. Remember, others will often come to Me when they see you modeling My character. Relax in Me, and I will help produce a godly spirit in you that reflects Me accurately.

From a Seeking Heart

Father, choosing my own way is such an easy habit to form. What I really want is to live in such a way that enables me to relate to others without condemning or copying ungodly standards. Extremes only beget trouble—unless I can be extreme in my desire to please You, extreme in my love for You, and extreme in my gentleness and thoughtfulness of others. I will choose Your control and Your ways, Lord. Today I will act with moderation.

Simple Truth

Make your first impression a divine impression.

DISCIPLINE

*No soldier on service gets entangled in civilian pursuits,
since his aim is to satisfy the one who enlisted him.*

2 TIMOTHY 2:4 RSV

FROM THE FATHER'S HEART

My child, I will help you develop discipline—a choice you can
make to keep balance in your life and to enable you to be
used more effectively in My kingdom. It is the constant desire to concentrate on the things that are important to Me
and to eliminate the things that are of no eternal value.
When you are disciplined, you will experience a godly power
that spreads into every area of your life.

FROM A SEEKING HEART

Father, I have never regretted "enlisting" in Your army. But
there are times when I feel like anything but a soldier. In those
moments, instead of going AWOL, I cry out to You, Lord,
and purpose to follow Your orders with new determination.
Today I choose discipline for my life so that everything in me
will line up under Your command. You deserve that!

SIMPLE TRUTH
Few battles are won by one.

WORKMANSHIP

*We are God's workmanship,
created in Christ Jesus to do good works.*

EPHESIANS 2:10

FROM THE FATHER'S HEART

My child, because you are My workmanship, you can take pride in the One who has created you. I made you for My glory! You can trust Me as your Master Potter to smooth the rough edges of your life in order to make you useful to Me. Shaping you into My special vessel is a joy to Me.

FROM A SEEKING HEART

Father, I was cracked and flawed; yet You loved me, believed in me, and took time to reshape me in Your image. When I'm tempted to feel inferior or fear that I'll be shelved for poor performance, I think about the patient work You've done to make me who I am today. Lord, I am Your workmanship, Your special creation, and through Your love I choose to live out the divine purpose for which You created me.

SIMPLE TRUTH

God specializes in original creations.

OPTIMISM

Whatever is true, whatever is honorable,
whatever is just, whatever is pure, whatever is lovely,
whatever is gracious, if there is any excellence,
if there is anything worthy of praise,
think about these things.

PHILIPPIANS 4:8 RSV

FROM THE FATHER'S HEART

My child, you will find that optimism comes when you set your heart and eyes on Me instead of the circumstances around you. Optimism helps you deliberately try to choose the good and positive in life and in other people, not negating reality, but opting to believe that with God all things are possible.

FROM A SEEKING HEART

Lord, from the time my eyes first greet Your morning, I want to think of You. Let praise fill my mind and heart as I give the day to You. Drive away any complaining spirit. Replace any negative thoughts with pictures You create for me in Your Word and through Your example. Lord, instead of believing the worst, I choose to see the best—and concentrate on the good You want to bring out of every situation and circumstance.

SIMPLE TRUTH

Pessimism sees negative reality; optimism sees positive possibility.

ESTEEM

"Love each other as I have loved you."

JOHN 15:12

FROM THE FATHER'S HEART

My child, you will find true esteem when you understand that I love you deeply, forgive you totally, and accept you unconditionally. You have value and worth as My child. Rest in My perfection and grace, knowing that nothing you do can change My love for you. The knowledge that I love you will free you to value others in the same way as I value you.

FROM A SEEKING HEART

Father, too much introspection and too little inspection of Your incredible love can lead me at times into the lie that I am worthless. How can I love others if I am focusing on my own inabilities instead of Your possibilities? Today I'm choosing esteem—to accept myself as a deeply loved and acceptable child of God. Is there anyone who is struggling today, Lord? Let me add value to her or his life by showing that person Your strong love.

SIMPLE TRUTH

Anything good in us is only because of the good in Him.

PROGRESSIVENESS

Search me, O God, and know my heart. . . .
See if there is any offensive way in me.

PSALM 139:23–24

FROM THE FATHER'S HEART

My child, when you give Me the freedom to amend your life and activities to fit My divine agenda, you are learning progressiveness. Holding on to unnecessary baggage will only prevent your moving forward. Progressiveness involves the willingness to exchange your outgrown habits, comfort, and attitudes for the greater work of My kingdom.

FROM A SEEKING HEART

Lord, in the home of my heart are so many "comfort" stations—places where I neither move backward nor forward—but stay the same. Maybe it's easier not to move. Maybe fear immobilizes me at times. Turn Your searchlight on those areas, Lord. Light up the path that I might see Your footprints and walk in them. I cannot live on yesterday's inspiration. Today is a new day—and I choose progressiveness, so I can move forward boldly with You, Lord.

SIMPLE TRUTH

Looking backward helps if it shows us how far we've come—and how far we still need to go.

NEATNESS

Your beauty. . .should be that of your inner self,
the unfading beauty of a gentle and quiet spirit.

1 PETER 3:3–4

FROM THE FATHER'S HEART

My child, adorning your inner spirit with outward simplicity
helps you develop neatness. Your outer shell is unimportant,
but when you frame it neatly and attractively, making the best
of what I have given to you, you can enhance, not detract,
from My beauty within you. You will never go wrong when
you remember to adorn yourself for My glory alone.

FROM A SEEKING HEART

Lord, no matter what I wear, I want to look like You! I may
not feel attractive; I may not turn any heads. But You have
given me designer genes that fit me perfectly. Instead of
worrying about my outer appearance, I will concentrate on
simple neatness, so the inner You can shine through me!

SIMPLE TRUTH

We're always dressed for success when we wear His
robes of righteousness.

TACTFULNESS

If possible, so far as it depends upon you,
live peaceably with all.

ROMANS 12:18 RSV

FROM THE FATHER'S HEART

My child, as you learn to treat others with the same dignity and respect that I do, you will learn more about tactfulness. All people are of value to Me and deserve your care and kindness so they can see My character through you. Choose to work peaceably among all, and let Me control your thoughts and feelings. With tactfulness, you can help others rather than hinder their spiritual growth. Speak My mind, not yours.

FROM A SEEKING HEART

Father, instead of tactfulness, sometimes I feel like I have the gift of "blurt." Like the apostle Paul, I say what I don't mean to say and don't say what I should say. But when my focus is on You and others, You will direct every conversation and control every relationship. With You, I need not nurture a "foot-in-mouth" disorder. You always treated others tactfully and with respect. I choose to do the same.

SIMPLE TRUTH

Open mouth; insert Christ's words.

FRUGALITY

*"Give me neither poverty nor riches,
but give me only my daily bread."*

PROVERBS 30:8

FROM THE FATHER'S HEART

My child, choosing to limit your desires in order to make your life readily accessible to My work is a part of frugality. I'm not asking you to beg for crumbs or hoard stale manna but to learn to be content with My daily provision, using well what I give you and trusting Me for each day's needs. I am not a stingy God. I love to bless My children, especially when they are good stewards.

FROM A SEEKING HEART

Father, when my wants exceed my needs, You remind me of what's really important. I need so little—yet You give me so much. Your example of frugality motivates me to act accordingly. You owned it all; yet You gave up everything, denying Yourself the luxuries that would only hinder Your goals. I want nothing more than the rich joy of Your daily presence. I will act with frugality, because You meet all my needs.

SIMPLE TRUTH

Little is much when God multiplies it.

VERSATILITY

And I said, "Here am I. Send me!"

ISAIAH 6:8

FROM THE FATHER'S HEART

My child, I will develop versatility in you when you refuse to close the door to any area where I want to use you. Allow Me to develop and bless whatever talents or abilities I have given you. It may seem illogical to you, and you may wonder why I'm choosing a certain direction for you. But your willingness to go wherever I send you means you are trusting Me for what is best.

FROM A SEEKING HEART

Father, it is not my job to question Your ways. You open doors, and You close doors. You used versatility throughout Your Word as You called people to different tasks. I need to be willing to change directions anytime I hear Your call—even if it makes no sense to me at the time. My heart is open, Lord. I'm listening for Your voice.

SIMPLE TRUTH

God is more interested in our commitment than our comfort.

TRANSPARENCY

O LORD, you have searched me and you know me. . . .
You are familiar with all my ways.

PSALM 139:1, 3

FROM THE FATHER'S HEART

My child, I develop transparency in you when you allow Me
the privilege of making Myself at home in your life. You need
not be afraid of the pain of disclosure. I created you, and I already know everything about you. But when you release the
rooms of your heart to My lordship, I will draw you near and
bring others into your life who need your touch.

FROM A SEEKING HEART

Lord, You know me so well. Nothing in my life is a surprise
to You. When I try to hide a corner of my heart, it is because there is darkness there—a difficult habit, an uncon-
fessed sin, a shadow from the past. Yet You own the key,
Lord, to all the rooms in my heart. Shine the light into
every nook and corner to diffuse any darkness. I choose to
live in transparency before You and others so my life can
truly reflect Your light in every room.

SIMPLE TRUTH

On our knees, darkness flees.

CLEVERNESS

*The plans of the mind belong to man,
but the answer of the tongue is from the LORD.*

PROVERBS 16:1 RSV

FROM THE FATHER'S HEART

My child, cleverness is not the deliberate twisting of some-one's mind to win them over to your ways. I will give you powerful words so you can use them to enlighten others about the message of Christ. Through the power of My Spirit, as you learn how to think My thoughts, I will trans-form your ideas so that others are persuaded, challenged, and inspired to draw closer to Me.

FROM A SEEKING HEART

Lord, I have tasted the futility of my own weak efforts. Speaking only my thoughts and words will make Your mes-sage fall on deaf ears. But as I focus on Your words and Your example, Your Spirit energizes me to speak God-given words with cleverness—not words that call attention to me but truths that set others free. Today I'll speak up for You—and leave the results to You.

SIMPLE TRUTH

God will add cleverness if we will add commitment.

VISION

Your ears will hear a voice behind you, saying,
"This is the way; walk in it."

ISAIAH 30:21

FROM THE FATHER'S HEART

My child, take time often to shut out all voices except Mine. As you keep your ears and eyes open to Me, I will give you vision and the ability to see the bigger picture of life. Is your God too small? When you listen to My voice rather than others, you can accomplish whatever I want through you. I will give you supernatural vision.

FROM A SEEKING HEART

Lord, You have X-ray vision. You can see the past, present, and future, and You know exactly what is waiting for me ahead. You can see straight into my heart. Your ears and eyes were always toward the Father, and You accomplished all He wanted You to do. Today I'm asking You to give me Your vision, Lord. How can I help others without it? I don't want to waste time with detours. I'm lost without Your leading, Lord.

SIMPLE TRUTH

Lord, give me eyes that see into the heart of Thee.

FRUITFULNESS

"I am the vine; you are the branches.
If a man remains in me and I in him, he will bear much fruit;
apart from me you can do nothing."

JOHN 15:5

FROM THE FATHER'S HEART

My child, fruitfulness will come when you are aware that any work apart from Me is useless. Place your weak branches into My hands, for I am your Living Vine, and My Father is the Gardener. When you allow My Father to prune away any straggling limbs and lift up any struggling ones, you can bear even more fruit.

FROM A SEEKING HEART

Lord, how foolish of me to strain in vain, as if my weak efforts would somehow mysteriously produce luscious fruit. The fruit I try to bear—love, joy, peace, patience, goodness—can only come from You. Father, prune away every dead and useless branch in me: every habit, every negative attitude, and every belief contrary to Your Word. I don't care what kind of fruit I bear—as long as it comes from You. I don't want to stand before You one day, barren of any lasting fruit. Today I choose Your fruitfulness.

SIMPLE TRUTH
Pruning isn't ruining.

AVAILABILITY

" 'Speak, LORD, for your servant is listening.' "

1 SAMUEL 3:9

FROM THE FATHER'S HEART

My child, throw away your own agendas. When you give Me permission to schedule your life the way I want to, without any interference, You will understand something about availability. Let your life be a blank page. As you release your time and your talents to Me, I will fill up those spaces and use you in a great way to touch the lives of others.

FROM A SEEKING HEART

Father, it seems like I am constantly in a struggle for time. The demands of life pull from every corner. In a tug-of-war vying for priorities, they cry out, "Clean me! Fix me! Teach me! Love me! Read me! Encourage me! Write me!" Yet when You call, Lord, I will drop my agendas and choose Yours. Nothing is more important than Your plans, Lord. Here is my clean page; write on it what You wish. Lord, I'm available.

SIMPLE TRUTH
Availability is far better than "failability."

PASSION

As the deer pants for streams of water,
so my soul pants for you, O God.

PSALM 42:1

FROM THE FATHER'S HEART

My child, you will develop passion when you desire Me and everything about Me with your whole heart, soul, and mind. Passion results in a deep-down longing to know Me, to love Me, and to serve Me above all other pursuits. I have gifted you to experience and enjoy many things in your life that are good, but no passion should ever equal the love you have for Me.

FROM A SEEKING HEART

Lord, I've spent so much of my life chasing after passionate dreams, many of which are the dreams I felt You gave me. Yet often in the process, my pursuit of the dream surpassed my heart's passion for You. With every day that passes now, You give me a hunger that can only be filled by You, a thirst only You can quench. In everything You give me to do, may I serve with all my heart. But most of all, Lord, I want You to be my heart's true passion.

SIMPLE TRUTH

Never ration your passion for God.

ADAPTABILITY

*I have become all things to all men so that
by all possible means I might save some.*

1 CORINTHIANS 9:22

FROM THE FATHER'S HEART

My child, you will experience adaptability when you are willing to amend your own ideas for the greater good of another. There may be times when you will need to change your preferences but never your convictions, if they are truly based on My Word. Without Me, lasting change is impossible.

FROM A SEEKING HEART

Father, how foolish I am to hold on to old ideas and patterns when You are designing new avenues of opportunities for me. And sometimes the way You teach me is through the ideas of others. My preferences may be steeped in fear or tradition—or other comfortable roads I've always traveled. My convictions must always be centered in Your Word and the truth in it. Lord, I choose adaptability—any way You design it.

SIMPLE TRUTH

*Adaptability rarely comes by doing the same things
we've always done.*

LONG-SUFFERING

I urge you to live a life worthy of the calling you have received.
Be completely humble and gentle;
be patient, bearing with one another in love.

EPHESIANS 4:1–2

FROM THE FATHER'S HEART

My child, I will teach you long-suffering as you treat the hurts of others with the same tenderness that I show to you. My timetables are not the same as yours. My thoughts and ways are higher than yours. When you place the needs of others above your own and make yourself available to wait with them in love, others will see the fruits of My Spirit in your life and be drawn to Me.

FROM A SEEKING HEART

Lord, I look at You and see patience personified. You impartially and personally touched each one You met. Loving others was Your delight as You mirrored Your own Father's tenderness. Lord, lengthen my rope when the fuse is too short in my dealings with others. In light of all You've done and Your patience with me, I choose to be long-suffering with others.

SIMPLE TRUTH

A short fuse leads to quick explosions.

BEAUTY

The Spirit of the Lord GOD is upon me;
because the LORD hath anointed me to. . .
give unto them beauty for ashes, the oil of joy for mourning,
the garment of praise for the spirit of heaviness. . .

ISAIAH 61:1, 3 KJV

FROM THE FATHER'S HEART

My child, I will develop beauty in you when you give Me the privilege of sculpturing your life into My own masterpiece. Do not fear the sharpness of My chisel, for when I am through, you will be a true work of My heart. Real beauty recognizes that in My eyes, nothing is ever wasted.

FROM A SEEKING HEART

Lord, I've experienced the crushing of Your anvil and the reshaping by Your skilled hands. You are the Master Artist. Like a vase on the potter's wheel or a rose crushed in the hand of a gardener, may my life bear Your beauty marks and Your fragrance. Take the broken fragments of my life—the hurts, the pains, the disappointments, the failures—and make me a usable vessel for You. Lord, let Your beauty be seen in me.

SIMPLE TRUTH

Beauty is in the eyes of the Creator.

RESILIENCE

A righteous man falls seven times, and rises again.

PROVERBS 24:16 RSV

FROM THE FATHER'S HEART

My child, when you turn failure into victory, you are displaying resilience. You can choose to believe in My power rather than your own strength, knowing I will help you stand again with dignity and courage. Like a rubber ball, you will come bouncing back to Me with new resolve and purpose. I will use you to bless others, in spite of your weaknesses or difficult circumstances.

FROM A SEEKING HEART

Lord, no matter how many times I've fallen, You've restored me and set me on a straight path. When I'm tempted to turn aside, I see the Cross and Your life sacrificed for me in true selflessness. You put a new spring in my step and a longing in my heart to love You more and more. Lord, I choose resilience, and by faith I accept Your empowering to stand firm and to finish strong.

SIMPLE TRUTH

Falling does not always mean failing.

PRIDE

For great is the LORD and most worthy of praise.

PSALM 96:4

FROM THE FATHER'S HEART

My child, there is a difference between fleshly pride and the kind of pride I want you to feel. Good pride understands that the work I give you, no matter how great or small, is important to Me. Whatever you contribute to My kingdom deserves your best abilities and time, and it must be given to Me as a sacrifice of praise. A good father always takes pride in his child's work.

FROM A SEEKING HEART

Father, what an honor to work in Your kingdom! You have assigned me Your creative tasks, designed for me since birth. Forgive me for the times I did not understand the importance of even the smallest responsibility You gave me, times when I failed to see each encounter as a divine opportunity to make You known to others. I want to make our relationship my top priority. Lord, I choose to serve You with pride and with all the love in my heart for the One who has given so much for me.

SIMPLE TRUTH

No job is unimportant when we do it for Jesus.

LOVE

*Dear friends, let us love one another,
for love comes from God.
Everyone who loves has been born of God and knows God.*

1 JOHN 4:7

FROM THE FATHER'S HEART

My child, remember that love is a commitment. When you commit to value another in the same way that I value you, you are understanding more about how to love. It is a choice you can make to sacrifice your own wishes for the positive welfare of another, reaching out with gratitude to the One who first loved you. There is no sacrifice too great for the One you love.

FROM A SEEKING HEART

Father, everywhere I look there are people who need Your love—people with untold stories, people with heavy burdens, people with broken hearts. Putting myself first results only in selfishness and discontentment. But, Lord, when You empty me of self and fill my spirit with godly love, I see people through Your eyes. Today I choose to let Your love shine!

SIMPLE TRUTH
Love always has room for others.

EXTRAVAGANCE

*Mary took a pound of costly ointment of pure nard
and anointed the feet of Jesus and wiped his feet with her hair.*

JOHN 12:3 RSV

FROM THE FATHER'S HEART

My child, extravagance is what I did for you on the cross when I died for you. When you are extravagant, you are choosing second-mile love—the pouring out of love far beyond what is needed, expected, or deserved. It is lavishing upon Me and others that which I value most highly, regardless of the cost.

FROM A SEEKING HEART

Lord, I have never known or felt such extravagant love as I have from You. When Your love fills me to overflowing, something happens that I cannot explain. Suddenly, fresh ideas and caring behaviors appear on the screen of my imagination and beg to be lavished on others. Lord, instead of choosing inexpensive gifts, I will watch for opportunities to give costly gifts—thoughtful gifts and deeds motivated by godly, extravagant love. Today I will start with one who is totally undeserving—just like You did for me.

SIMPLE TRUTH

God "emptied His pockets" when He gave us His Son, Jesus.

SELF-CONTROL

For this very reason,
make every effort to add to your faith goodness;
and to goodness, knowledge; and to knowledge, self-control.

2 PETER 1:5–6

FROM THE FATHER'S HEART

My child, are you ready for change in your life? Are you tired of the same old patterns? When you learn to agree with Me about areas of weakness in your life and deny your own selfish desires in exchange for My best, I love to fill you with My Spirit's self-control. Let Me control your life, and I will help you surrender areas that are harmful to yourself and others.

FROM A SEEKING HEART

Lord, my heart longs for the day when Christians will no longer struggle over negative voices and issues that demand our attention daily. I am learning that self-control is impossible without God-control. I am Your child, Lord, dead to sin and harmful habits. Remind me of that often, so that I will not waste my time trying to become someone I already am. I choose to fortify the walls of my defenses daily and to exercise Your control over my life. Only then can I live with peace and contentment.

SIMPLE TRUTH

Gaining even one victory gives us courage to pursue
self-control in other areas.

CHASTITY

Do you not know that your body is a temple of the Holy Spirit,
who is in you, whom you have received from God?

1 CORINTHIANS 6:19

FROM THE FATHER'S HEART

My child, would you dump garbage onto a spotless floor?
Would you try to destroy something that I have called My
temple? Recognizing that your body belongs to Me and that
it is the home of My Spirit will motivate you to choose
chastity as a part of your godly character. It is a conscious
desire to please Me rather than yourself. I love you and want
to protect you from anything that would harm what I have
so lovingly created.

FROM A SEEKING HEART

Lord, I long to be that pure place where You will feel comfortable anytime day or night. Come and make my heart
Your home! Come and make this temple a place of honor, a
place of purity, a place where shame has been destroyed by
Your forgiveness, a place where chastity is a part of all I
think or feel or see or do. I will be Your temple, Lord.

SIMPLE TRUTH

Hearts, like homes, need continual spring-cleaning.

SWEETNESS

For we are unto God a sweet savour of Christ,
in them that are saved, and in them that perish.

2 CORINTHIANS 2:15 KJV

FROM THE FATHER'S HEART

My child, you may question why I allow you to be crushed and broken. But when you smell the sweet fragrance coming from your life, you will understand more. Others will notice, too. When you enter a room, the sweetness of heaven's perfume will linger long after you leave—because My presence will be there, too. Submit to My will, and trust Me. I will bring good out of all things.

FROM A SEEKING HEART

Lord, even the most expensive perfumes cannot match the fragrance of You. Remove any bitter tears or hangover fears from the past. I want sweetness in my life—to be a fragrance of Your life to those around me. I want to be like You, Jesus. I know You will allow into my life only what will conform me to Your image. Whatever it costs to wear Your perfume, I know it will be an eternal investment. I choose sweetness, Lord, because I choose You.

SIMPLE TRUTH

When we wear His perfume daily, the fragrance
never dies.

CHARISMA

*Everyone was filled with awe, and many wonders
and miraculous signs were done by the apostles.*

ACTS 2:43

FROM THE FATHER'S HEART

My child, in yourself you can do nothing. But when you
surrender your life to Me, I will empower you. Then you
will feel the effects of charisma, the glow of My Spirit
drawing people to Me as you let My light shine through
you. How I manifest Myself to you is My decision. But
when you are sold out to me and willing to wait for My
power, there is no limit to what I can do through your life.
Others will see—and take note—that you have been with Me.

FROM A SEEKING HEART

Lord, You have told us we would do even greater works
than You. You exemplified charisma, as people were drawn
to You constantly. I am only an ordinary vessel, Lord, in love
with an extraordinary God. Help me access by faith that
which You have already given me so others can see Your
charisma in me. Lord, shine brightly in my life!

SIMPLE TRUTH

*We're not here to dazzle others—but to shine for
Christ.*

BRAVERY

"Now then, be strong and brave."

2 SAMUEL 2:7

FROM THE FATHER'S HEART

My child, you may not feel like moving beyond your own comfort zone, but when you do it for the welfare of others, you will understand something of bravery. Your strength and knowledge are limited, but you can rely on My power, even in seemingly impossible situations. Will you trust Me today? I see in you a brave warrior!

FROM A SEEKING HEART

Lord, on earth You lived far beyond Your comfort zone, and You even chose death so that I could have life. Lord, let Your Spirit infuse me daily with a spirit of bravery that can, in time, help others find confidence and courage in You as well. I refuse to hide in closets of timidity or fear when You have clothed me with the armor of Christ. Today I choose bravery, Lord.

SIMPLE TRUTH
Don't waver—be braver.

LEADERSHIP

*"Whoever wants to become great among you
must be your servant."*

Matthew 20:26

From the Father's Heart

My child, you can develop leadership by becoming a servant
and concentrating on the creative potential in others. As
you work to meet the needs of those around you, I will give
you the strength and resources to accomplish My tasks. Just
as I focused on My Father's will, you must keep your eyes
on Me and your heart bowed before Me. Those who lead
carry a towel with them at all times.

From a Seeking Heart

Lord, forgive me for the times my heart craved greatness
instead of servanthood. I can only lead as I follow Your
example—not a hand-washing Pharisee but a foot-washing
servant. Others need You desperately. Lord, let me lead
them to You with a true servant's spirit of leadership.

Simple Truth

True leaders are simply good followers. . .of Jesus.

Day 53

AUTHORITY

*I urge, then, first of all, that requests, prayers, intercession
and thanksgiving be made for everyone—for kings and all
those in authority, that we may live peaceful and quiet lives.*

1 TIMOTHY 2:1–2

FROM THE FATHER'S HEART

My child, I have equipped you with bold authority—true,
God-given power to lead, teach, or serve in a way that will
honor Me. Recognize that I am your ultimate power source,
but be willing to submit to the ones I have placed over you
for your own protection. As long as you stay under My um-
brella of protection, I can work freely in your life.

FROM A SEEKING HEART

Lord, I do not want to shirk my responsibilities or cower under
overwhelming tasks. You have given Your children heaven's
authority to live as kings and queens; yet we often choose the
life of paupers. No matter how big or small my work is, may I
use Your authority, the name of Jesus, well—always with a
servant's heart. I choose not to use this authority as an opportunity to lord it over another—but to first submit myself to
You and to respect the positions of those in authority over me.

SIMPLE TRUTH
*It is harder to "come under" than to "climb over" an-
other's authority.*

FORGIVENESS

*Above all, love each other deeply,
because love covers over a multitude of sins.*

1 PETER 4:8

FROM THE FATHER'S HEART

My child, through forgiveness you can cover the faults of
others with My love and affirm them with the same grace I
have shown to you. Do you still remember the first time you
knew you were forgiven? My grace covered all your sins—
warts and all—because I loved you. Nothing can change
that forgiveness—past, present, and future. I will give you
the grace to forgive others as well. You will inherit a blessing when you do.

FROM A SEEKING HEART

Father, I lost count of the "seventy times seven" times You
have forgiven me. Remind me often, lest I forget how deep
and how complete Your forgiveness is. Others are watching
Christians to see if our love mirrors Yours—if we can truly
forgive them, especially when they don't deserve it and by
those who have wounded us so deeply. In the same spirit in
which You forgive me, Lord, I choose to make forgiveness a
lifelong habit.

SIMPLE TRUTH

Forgiveness remembers—to forget.

ZEALOUSNESS

"I am. . .zealous for God as you all are this day."

ACTS 22:3 RSV

FROM THE FATHER'S HEART

My child, zealousness characterizes those who know Me. This impassioned desire for Me comes when you choose wisely where you will place your energies and become excited about the tasks I give you. I am always working through you to accomplish My good purpose and pleasure for your life. You can be zealous about many things, but concentrate on what is lasting, My child.

FROM A SEEKING HEART

Father, it is easy to become excited about things that really don't have any eternal value: a new home, a job promotion, or educational accomplishments. And these are fine. But if they replace our zealousness for You and Your work, then we have misplaced our joy. Lord, today I recognize that of all the things I treasure the most, You are the most valuable. Make every moment an eternal one as I invest my time in You and in others, Lord. I want to be zealous for You, God!

SIMPLE TRUTH

> *Our checkbooks and our calendars usually tell the truth about our priorities.*

DIVERSITY

There are diversities of operations,
but it is the same God which worketh all in all.

1 CORINTHIANS 12:6 KJV

FROM THE FATHER'S HEART

My child, I planned My world with diversity. No two creatures are alike. Accept your uniqueness in Christ as I created you. In My body on earth, the church—believers everywhere—there is no room for envy or misunderstanding. When you can allow Me to use your differences and your unique gifts to build up and bless others for My glory, you are developing the quality of diversity. My children all serve the same God.

FROM A SEEKING HEART

Father, we have not all been given the same task or the same genes or gifts to accomplish those tasks. Forgive me when I expect others to act like me or think like me, without taking the time to understand Your methods of diversity. At the same time, I recognize that even though You develop that uniqueness about us—diversity—we all still need to operate with the mind of Christ and work for Your glory. Just as You were diverse in Your dealings with others, I must be also.

SIMPLE TRUTH

In God's eyes, there is no such thing as a twin
personality. Each of us is unique.

EXPERIENCE

Tribulation worketh patience;
and patience, experience; and experience, hope.

ROMANS 5:3–4 KJV

FROM THE FATHER'S HEART

My child, you will develop experience by submitting yourself to My school of life as a learner, listening carefully to My instructions. Approach every opportunity in life as a potential lesson from Me, and choose to pass on to others what you have already learned. That experience will then translate into wisdom if you place it into My hands and let Me teach you My purpose through that and every lesson.

FROM A SEEKING HEART

Lord, whether I am young or old, I want godly experience to characterize my life. I have not always looked for Your purpose and Your lessons in every situation, especially in the ordinary, day-to-day events—or maybe even in the hard times. I want to build a legacy for my children, grandchildren, and for other disciples who need my life's experience.

SIMPLE TRUTH

The kind of legacies we leave depends on the kind of
lives we live.

HUMOR

A cheerful heart is good medicine.

PROVERBS 17:22

FROM THE FATHER'S HEART

My child, the ability to laugh at yourself and at life without hurting others characterizes a true sense of humor. With laughter, you can oil the hinges of others' lives—where doors creak with bitterness, sadness, and depression—and add a touch of sunshine. The world is too full of sadness. It needs My special love—and a healthy dose of joy. Smile often. You'll find that humor makes healthier bodies and spirits.

FROM A SEEKING HEART

Lord, Your sense of humor is evident when I look around at all Your creation—so many kinds of creatures of all shapes and all sizes. And when I think of You blessing children while You were on earth, I picture the crinkles in Your face and the twinkle in Your eyes. Everywhere You traveled, You touched lives, restoring joy and laughter. So many need that joy in their lives, Lord. Use me as an instrument of humor to lighten the loads of others. I choose to laugh, not complain.

SIMPLE TRUTH

A smile a day keeps a frown away.

COOPERATION

We are labourers together with God.

1 CORINTHIANS 3:9 KJV

FROM THE FATHER'S HEART

My child, I love it when you exercise cooperation and place a higher priority on the success of My work than on your own desires. That willingness to work together with others for the good of My kingdom shows Me you are serious about making a difference with the gifts and abilities I have given you. I will bless that cooperative spirit—the work of your heart—*and* the work of your hands.

FROM A SEEKING HEART

Lord, it's not always easy to work alongside others when we are all so different. Yet when the common goal is to please and honor You, what a joy it is to see the end result! I will work together with others, Lord, remembering that it is You who works in us to accomplish Your good will and pleasure. Teach me that spirit of cooperation that wants to elevate Your work above my own.

SIMPLE TRUTH

A winning team—Takes Every Available Messenger.

FLUENCY

The words of a man's mouth are deep waters,
but the fountain of wisdom is a bubbling brook.

PROVERBS 18:4

FROM THE FATHER'S HEART

My child, do not use Moses' excuse and tell Me you cannot speak well. I will give you fluency—the ability to make words come to life in order to encourage, inspire, or motivate others. I will use your talents to speak for Me if you will choose to train and develop that gift and let Me fill you with My inspiration. The convincing depends on My Spirit, not on you. All I want is your willingness and availability.

FROM A SEEKING HEART

Father, sometimes I feel more like a babbling stream than a bubbling brook. Nevertheless, I trust You to put the words in my mouth at the right time. I will prepare well so that I can be ready to speak about You whenever You say the word. When You energize me with Your Spirit, my words will flow with wisdom and grace. It's a joy to share about You, Lord. Let the Spirit flow!

SIMPLE TRUTH

When God blesses, our words are like manna from heaven to hungry souls.

COMPOSURE

"In quietness and trust is your strength."

ISAIAH 30:15

FROM THE FATHER'S HEART

My child, I will give you composure as your spirit is at rest in Me. Remember to rely on Me alone, and refuse to look at your circumstances. You will sink every time if you look at the stormy seas and not at Me. When you place your trust in Me, I will fill you with inner strength—and others will wonder how you can remain so calm.

FROM A SEEKING HEART

Lord, You always had composure. Even the winds and the waves quieted in awe of Your strength and power. In Your thoughts and reactions, You never wavered, even when You faced death. I want that same peaceful spirit of composure, Lord. The next time I am tempted to let my problems consume me, I will remember Your example and find strength in You. I choose to trust You and to rest in You as I walk by faith, not by sight!

SIMPLE TRUTH

None of us can "hold it together" all the time, but He can.

WORTHINESS

I may. . .be found in him, not having a righteousness of my own, based on law, but that which is through faith in Christ, the righteousness from God that depends on faith.

PHILIPPIANS 3:8–9 RSV

FROM THE FATHER'S HEART

My child, worthiness is a gift I give you based not on your own value but on My righteousness. You can dress in fine clothing and act like a prince or princess, but it will not make you worthy to earn My pleasure. Only as you choose by faith to make Me your Lord will I declare you complete in My sight. That's when you become a King's kid. It is *whose* you are and *who* I am that make you worthy.

FROM A SEEKING HEART

Lord, I remember the times when I thought my own actions would net me an A+ in Your sight and earn Your heavenly favor. I also remember the futile thinking that I could never do anything to please such a perfect God. But, Lord, You are not a perfectionist. You are a loving God who planned Jesus' death and resurrection as a prerequisite for worthiness when we place our faith in Him. I am tired of trying to be someone I already am. Lord, thank You for this gift of worthiness. I will wear it humbly and gratefully.

SIMPLE TRUTH

I will be the me You say I am.

EMPATHY

*Rejoice with them that do rejoice,
and weep with them that weep.*

ROMANS 12:15 KJV

FROM THE FATHER'S HEART

My child, when you feel the deepest hurts and needs of others as if they were your own, you are developing empathy. As you make yourself available to Me, I will make your heart tender toward those who need comfort, encouragement, and strength. Remember how I wiped away your tears as your Abba Father, and you will understand how to minister to others in the same way.

FROM A SEEKING HEART

Lord, how deeply You felt others' hurts! How completely You met their needs! Help me never to offer empty phrases or pat answers on a platter of Christian ignorance and insensitivity. Rather, Lord, allow me to put myself in their shoes if I have not walked there, and let Your Spirit fill me with a deep sense of empathy. I want to understand, Lord. I want to be Your arms that reach out with love and comfort to others.

SIMPLE TRUTH

A hug brings heaven a little closer to our hearts.

ELASTICITY

*Create in me a pure heart, O God,
and renew a steadfast spirit within me.*

PSALM 51:10

FROM THE FATHER'S HEART

My child, are you willing to be stretched beyond your normal limitations? Do you have a desire to bounce back after failure or trials? Then let Me give you elasticity. Don't be afraid of the things you don't understand. Look to Me as your source of strength. I will bring renewal and hope to your heart once again. When you feel like you are breaking, remember, you are only bending.

FROM A SEEKING HEART

Father, there are times when I have felt like a rubber band stretched too thin, about to snap. But even in the most difficult situations, or when the fault is mine, I can trust You for elasticity. I am no longer afraid of being broken. If You stretch me more than what I feel is my capability, it is to show Yourself mighty and cause me to rely on You even more. You will accomplish Your good will for my life, Lord. I'll be Your elastic rubber band.

SIMPLE TRUTH
Bending often comes before sending.

ALERTNESS

Be on your guard; stand firm in the faith;
be men of courage; be strong.

1 CORINTHIANS 16:13

FROM THE FATHER'S HEART

My child, your enemy plots daily how he can thwart your
successes and My plans for you. You must constantly be on
guard, and be ready to fend off his attacks. If you will depend on My strength rather than your own, I will give you
alertness. My Spirit and My Word will make you aware of
your humanness and help you choose to ready yourself for
the inevitable battles that face you daily.

FROM A SEEKING HEART

Lord, You never turned aside from Your earthly tasks. Although constantly attacked, You remained steadfast and
alert. Lord, steady my shaky feet. With Your help, I will
bring captive every deceptive thought, and I'll obey the holy
checks from Your Spirit each time my enemy is in my
neighborhood. I want to be prepared for battle—and not
wait until temptation comes to try to rally my scrambled defenses. Lord, I choose alertness—day in and day out—to
listen to and heed Your warnings.

SIMPLE TRUTH

Never face danger as a lone ranger.

ABSTINENCE

Abstain from sinful desires, which war against your soul.

1 PETER 2:11

FROM THE FATHER'S HEART

My child, Christianity is not a list of dos and don'ts. But I have given you freedom to choose what is right. You have My Word as a standard and My example to follow. Make the deliberate choice of abstinence from harmful things as you put Me first rather than bow to the pressures of others. By participating only in those activities that will keep you pure and honor Christ, you can be a witness to others.

FROM A SEEKING HEART

Lord, I don't need others to write me a code of ethics. You already did that in Your Word. Help me to interpret it accurately and with grace and love determine what will bring You honor and glory in my life. You have given me freedom of choice, but when there are situations or activities that would compromise my character in Christ and bring harm to myself or others, I will choose abstinence.

SIMPLE TRUTH

Peer pressure is usually fear *pressure.*

CONTINUITY

*Continue in what you have learned and have firmly believed,
knowing from whom you learned it.*

2 TIMOTHY 3:14 RSV

FROM THE FATHER'S HEART

My child, do you struggle with doing right at times? I will
give you continuity and help keep your faith active, alive,
and effective. Remember the lessons you've learned, and
renew your determination to allow no separations between
your actions and your beliefs. Trust Me to help you walk the
walk and talk the talk. Still wondering how? Just show up in
My presence every day—and I will take over from there.

FROM A SEEKING HEART

Lord, everything You did spelled continuity—in Your purpose, Your teaching, and Your love for people. You never al-
tered Your purpose during Your life on earth. You know my
weaknesses, but I know Your strength. With Your help, I will
close the gap between what I say I believe and what I actively
do. I choose continuity as I learn from You, my Master
Teacher.

SIMPLE TRUTH

*God's Spirit will keep you growing and growing and
growing.*

JOVIALITY

A merry heart hath a continual feast.

PROVERBS 15:15 KJV

FROM THE FATHER'S HEART

My child, I love it when you see the light side of life by taking one day at a time. That quality of joviality, of refusing to make yourself a slave to worry, will help you lighten up and enjoy each day as a gift from Me to you. Once you make joviality a habit, you'll feast every day on the joy of life, on loving others, and on knowing Me as your Friend and Father.

FROM A SEEKING HEART

Father, life is too short for me to live in the past or the future. And life is too precious for me to miss the sweet times You've planned for my life daily. Like daily capsules, I will absorb the quality of joviality to keep me from taking myself too seriously, and I'll use it to lighten another's burden. And with great joy I will come into Your presence daily and feast on Your love and goodness.

SIMPLE TRUTH

Don't live tomorrow, today. Don't live today, tomorrow. Enjoy today, today.

POLITENESS

Love is patient, love is kind. . . . It is not rude.

1 Corinthians 13:4–5

From the Father's Heart

My child, when you understand that every person is a special creation, how else can you treat another except with politeness? You demonstrate the love I have given to you as you respect the rights and privileges of others. Your treatment of others in this way says volumes about your character—and that you belong to Me.

From a Seeking Heart

Lord, when I'm tempted to respond with rudeness, help me to refrain from fleshly actions. Whether I see red lights, yellow lights, flashing lights, broken lights, or no lights at all does not matter. Injustice, delay, or inefficiency still demands politeness and courtesy. I am Your child, and others are watching closely to see if I will respond in love or irritation. Lord, I choose politeness because I know You would, too.

Simple Truth

People may not remember what happened, but they will remember how we respond.

TRUTHFULNESS

I have chosen the way of truth;
I have set my heart on your laws.

PSALM 119:30

FROM THE FATHER'S HEART

My child, many will come to you claiming to know the truth. But underneath their words you will find a slippery lining of deceit. Truthfulness comes by setting your heart on what I say is right. My Word is truth. You will discover what is right when you meditate on its message daily. Truthfulness is a conscious effort to make My ways known, leaving the consequences in My hands.

FROM A SEEKING HEART

Lord, You indeed spoke truth; and many disputed Your words, disagreeing with Your life, Your actions, and Your purpose. I can trust You, for You are Truth. Your Word will drive out any unnecessary fear I may encounter in declaring Your truth to others. I will be a witness to what I know and what You have taught me, Lord. I choose truthfulness, not deception, in all my dealings with others—and especially with You.

SIMPLE TRUTH

Jesus is the whole Truth and nothing but the Truth.

HUMILITY

Clothe yourselves with humility toward one another,
because, "God opposes the proud but gives grace to the humble."

1 PETER 5:5

FROM THE FATHER'S HEART

My child, don't worry about those who climb the ladder by
stepping on the rungs of others' feelings and rights. You are
different because you have My nature. As you surrender
your rights of ownership to Me, I will develop My quality
of humility in you. I will help you consider others more important than yourself and remind you often that when good
comes from you, it is because of the One who lives in you.

FROM A SEEKING HEART

Lord, if You could surrender all Your rights and kingship, I
can yield my rights to any claim on what I call *my* things.
You own it all, Lord, and I am only a caretaker and servant
in Your kingdom. As an act of faith, I will daily remove any
outdated clothes of pride and don the clothing of humility—that I might be in a position to mirror Your heart and
character daily. Because there is no good in me without You,
I cannot do this alone. I depend on Your Spirit each day to
fill me with Your grace and humility.

SIMPLE TRUTH

Humility is not a "You-melody" but a "Him-melody."

ENDURANCE

*Consider him who endured such opposition from sinful men,
so that you will not grow weary and lose heart.*

HEBREWS 12:3

FROM THE FATHER'S HEART

My child, should you find yourself off course, ask yourself, "Who or what caused me to turn aside?" It was not Me. I will help you run with endurance—the ability to stay focused on one goal until its completion. Keep your eyes on Me, and refuse to let the events around you or the emotions within you to distract you. Weariness comes when you try to run the race in your own strength or when you start looking at the wrong goal. Run with endurance. I have a crown waiting for you at the finish line.

FROM A SEEKING HEART

Lord, no matter how many times I have fallen, You have always picked me up and put me back on course. At times I am so eager to finish the race because my bones and muscles and emotions cry, "Uncle." But I remember Your example, and I have set my heart on a path of endurance, Lord. I'm choosing to run this race well—with no shortcuts or detours—because I know You will see me through.

SIMPLE TRUTH

*The Lord is our great Reward. We must keep our eyes
on that goal alone.*

IMPARTIALITY

*My brothers, as believers in our glorious Lord Jesus Christ,
don't show favoritism.*

JAMES 2:1

FROM THE FATHER'S HEART

My child, how do you respond when someone different walks into the room? Are there any cliques in your circle of friends? Do you show any favoritism to your children or to others? I want you to exercise impartiality by choosing to honor every person as equal in My sight. You can add value to others by treating them with kindness and respect, just as I treat you.

FROM A SEEKING HEART

Lord, You truly love everyone the same. As You walked on earth, the thief, the leper, the priest, the child—all found a welcome place in Your heart. You have no favorites in Your kingdom. All are a part of Your family. I, too, desire impartiality in all my dealings with people. When there is discrepancy, Lord, show me the reason so I can correct the problem and make loving others a priority equal to Yours.

SIMPLE TRUTH
Preconceived notions rarely accompany impartiality.

FRESHNESS

As Christ was raised up from the dead
by the glory of the Father,
even so we also should walk in newness of life.

ROMANS 6:4 KJV

FROM THE FATHER'S HEART

My child, do you enjoy stale testimonies? Stagnant fountains? Programmed behavior? I want more for you than that. When you surrender your life to My control, I will give you freshness—a new way of attitude and action. Old habits die hard, but in Me you are a new creation. I will change your old habits and give you a new perspective on life.

FROM A SEEKING HEART

Lord, the same power that raised You from the dead raises us up from sinful habits, attitudes, and behaviors when we put our trust in You. I'm weary of fighting old sinful patterns that should have been destroyed long ago. I choose freshness, Lord. To walk in that newness of life and live victoriously every day as a fresh testimony of Your grace—this is my desire.

SIMPLE TRUTH

Growing old should not mean growing stale.

OPENNESS

Confess your faults one to another, and pray one for another.

JAMES 5:16 KJV

FROM THE FATHER'S HEART

My child, others do not have My X-ray vision. They cannot see into your heart like I can. You could fool them but not Me. However, I hope you will always choose openness and be willing to let others see your life as it really is. Let Me help you release the mistakes of your past and welcome the support of others in determining your future. As My child, you have nothing to hide.

FROM THE FATHER'S HEART

Lord, it's always easier to hide behind a charade of busyness, weariness, or fear; but You desire truth in our inmost parts. As we open our lives to others, maybe we can encourage others to open up their lives to You, too. I choose—and need—others' support and prayers, Lord, to help me grow more and more like You. And, Lord, my heart's door is always open to You.

SIMPLE TRUTH

Shame has no room to grow in an open house.

DEPENDENCY

And my God will supply every need of yours
according to his riches in glory in Christ Jesus.

PHILIPPIANS 4:19 RSV

FROM THE FATHER'S HEART

My child, has there ever been a need I did not supply for
you? Have I ever abandoned you? I own the world and
everything in it. I can only meet your needs as you abandon
your own self-will and declare your dependency on Me as a
Sovereign God. A spirit of dependency does not demand to
know answers ahead of time, nor does it question the ability of the Giver. Like a little child, keep your heart on Me,
take My hand, and walk by faith—not by sight.

FROM A SEEKING HEART

Father, every year I realize how truly dependent on You I
must be. To question Your ability to meet my needs would be
to reduce You to a pauper. Everything I have belongs to You;
You have provided it for my enjoyment and need. I remember
too well the result of an independent spirit. Trying to live
apart from You, Lord, is like trying to breathe without air. You
are everything to me, and I depend on You for life!

SIMPLE TRUTH

Dependency does not mean depend-on-me. God helps
those who depend on Him.

NONCONFORMITY

Be not conformed to this world:
but be ye transformed by the renewing of your mind.

ROMANS 12:2 KJV

FROM THE FATHER'S HEART

My child, others will always try to squeeze you into molds
of their own choosing. Nonconformity is the willingness to
let Me change things around you rather than your fitting an
ungodly, prescribed mold. You can deliberately choose to
run from what is harmful and to let Me transform your life
into what I designed for you before you even uttered your
first birth cry. I have a beautiful purpose for you—one that
will bring much glory to Me—and much joy to you.

FROM A SEEKING HEART

Lord, if anyone challenged the norms of the day, You did. If
anyone failed to fit the expectations and standards of others,
You did. Separate and holy, You left a perfect pattern for me
to follow. I cannot change anyone's behavior; I cannot even
change my own. But You have—and You will—keep trans-
forming my life so I can make a positive influence wherever
You choose to send me. Here I am, Lord. Change me even
more.

SIMPLE TRUTH

*Some people live to make a statement. Others live to
make a difference.*

CHEERFULNESS

A happy heart makes the face cheerful.

PROVERBS 15:13

FROM THE FATHER'S HEART

My child, I love it when you let a cheerful attitude place the needs of others before your own needs. I am not asking for a syrupy denial of reality but a deliberate choice to be happy in all circumstances. With My help, you can be yourself while consciously trying to see the best in life and My hand in everything. Even your face will know the difference.

FROM A SEEKING HEART

Father, no one likes to hang around complainers—and I don't want to be one, either. When You have given me everything I will ever need in this life for contentment, how can I possibly focus on my own temporary discomfort or problems? If cheerfulness is contagious, I'd like to start an epidemic by sharing Your joy daily.

SIMPLE TRUTH

Why be of good cheer? Because Jesus is here!

SPONTANEITY

*I will praise you as long as I live,
and in your name I will lift up my hands.*

PSALM 63:4

FROM THE FATHER'S HEART

My child, I love to see you abandon yourself to Me as you enjoy My presence daily. I will continue to give you that unhindered freshness of spontaneity as you release your cares and fears to Me and respond to My touch on your life. Love Me and worship Me—like no one is watching you but Me.

FROM A SEEKING HEART

Lord, You are so worthy to be praised. And at times I am so overcome with emotion and joy that I feel like David, dancing unashamed before Your presence, head and heart lifted high. Let my joy know no bounds, Lord. Let my spirit rise to meet You and greet You with daily spontaneous offerings of praise and gratitude. I lift my hands and my heart to You always in pure devotion and adoration.

SIMPLE TRUTH

*Spiritual spontaneous combustion is when God lights
our fire for Him.*

TIMELINESS

Wait for the LORD.

PSALM 27:14

FROM THE FATHER'S HEART

My child, I know you may grow impatient to see My hand at work and to reap the results of answered prayer. But let timeliness have its work. Be willing to wait on My intervention before you act in any given situation. When you operate on My timetable, not your own, I will do far more than you could even imagine.

FROM A SEEKING HEART

Lord, You never ran ahead of Your heavenly Father's timetable. Even Your delays in personal ministry had an eternal purpose. I need that quality of timeliness, Lord. I may not understand the whys and the hows in my life, but I choose to trust You because I know You hold my future safely in Your hands. Today, Lord, I will wait on You.

SIMPLE TRUTH

Waiting is grating until we understand God's eternal purpose.

CHARITABLENESS

God is able to provide you with every blessing in abundance,
so that you... may provide in abundance for every good work.

2 CORINTHIANS 9:8 RSV

FROM THE FATHER'S HEART

My child, when you love others enough to share My goodness
in any circumstance, you are developing charitableness. That's
My plan of economy. I have blessed you with more than
enough so that you can, in turn, bless others—in the same way
I have blessed you. When the attitude of charitableness is operating in My children, no one should lack anything.

FROM A SEEKING HEART

Lord, I have learned that truly the best things are not
things. Too often in the past I have hoarded blessings for
myself, saving them for rainy-day needs. But, Lord, You
have blessed me too much for me to hold back anything
selfishly. I choose charitableness because I want to be a
blessing to others as You have been for me.

SIMPLE TRUTH

We are simply conduits of God's goodness.

CONFORMITY

That I may know him, and the power of his resurrection,
and the fellowship of his sufferings,
being made conformable unto his death.

PHILIPPIANS 3:10 KJV

FROM THE FATHER'S HEART

My child, lie still in the Potter's hands. I will not discard you; I have a wonderful plan for your life! I am always at work in you, seeking to make you like Me. I want your conformity, a willingness to exchange your life for My life, laying your own desires at My feet. Your desire to know Me above all other loves, regardless of the cost, means you are becoming conformed to My image. What a beautiful vessel you will be when I'm finished!

FROM A SEEKING HEART

Lord, the desire of my heart is to be like You—to act like You—and to truly be fashioned into the one You created me to be. Other activities may pull; other loves may pursue, but I choose to follow only that which will draw me into Your likeness. I understand being conformed to Your image will involve both the fellowship of Your presence and the fellowship of Your suffering. Grant me the strength to say no to all else but "Yes, Lord, yes!" to You.

SIMPLE TRUTH

We are safe in the hands of God.

TALENT

Whatever you do, do it all for the glory of God.

1 CORINTHIANS 10:31

FROM THE FATHER'S HEART

My child, I have given all My children talent—the raw materials of character I expect you to use for Me. Don't envy another's gift. This is My unique mark on your life that allows you to bless others with joy, encouragement, and inspiration. It is up to you to develop your talent in a way that will bring glory and honor to Me. I will always be there to help you, but you must be willing to work with Me and watch for divine opportunities to make a difference.

FROM A SEEKING HEART

Father, how You can take a lump of clay and bring beauty out of it is amazing. Fear drives us away from developing our potential at times; faith moves us forward because we want to make a difference. Comparison aborts our purpose; trust opens us to Your divine touch. Lord, for however long my life—and however great or small my talent—I will use it to make Your name famous.

SIMPLE TRUTH

> *Never envy the grass on the other side of the fence.*
> *Weeds probably grow there, too.*

AGILITY

Therefore, prepare your minds for action.

1 PETER 1:13

FROM THE FATHER'S HEART

My child, there are times when you must be still to hear My instructions. Tune out all other voices and just listen to Mine. Agility will come when your spirit is in tune with My Spirit. When you set your mind and heart on Me, you will hear My Spirit's "check" inside. As the check light comes on, you can then move quickly to do My will and accomplish My purpose for your life.

FROM A SEEKING HEART

Lord, there was never a time when You rebelled or moved ahead of Your Father. With great agility, You set out to accomplish well Your Father's plan. I, too, want to wait on You and prepare my heart for action. Lord, when the battle cry comes for offensive action, help me move with agility. The battle is Yours, Lord, but I will move quickly at Your voice.

SIMPLE TRUTH

The greatest battles begin in the mind.

GENUINENESS

"Let your light shine before men,
that they may see your good deeds
and praise your Father in heaven."

MATTHEW 5:16

FROM THE FATHER'S HEART

My child, are you willing to keep open house so that others can find Me? I will give you genuineness—the quality of a pure heart open to Me and to others. Then your desire will grow to let your life be a lighthouse for those in darkness, pointing the way to My intimate presence. Fake Christianity repels a seeker. What others want to see is the real thing.

FROM A SEEKING HEART

Lord, stoke the flickering flame in me and keep it burning brightly. As the true Light of the World, Lord, continue Your work of pushing out any corners of darkness in me so Your light can shine brightly. Then those who walk in the blackness of their own sinful habits, their hopelessness, or their disillusionments can find their way to You. I choose genuineness, and I will not hide this light, Lord. May my light—and my actions—always give praise to You.

SIMPLE TRUTH
People do not look for light in dark closets.

TRIUMPH

Now thanks be unto God,
which always causeth us to triumph in Christ.

2 Corinthians 2:14 kjv

From the Father's Heart

My child, don't let discouragement seep into your life and throw you off course. You will never move beyond what you think is possible, so believe in My power to accomplish anything through you. I will give you the ability to triumph— to see victory, regardless of the circumstances. Let Me fight your battles, and recognize that I have already won the greatest victory of all. You will never fail when you are on My side.

From a Seeking Heart

Lord, I choose to wear the clothes of a victor, not a loser. If I fall, I will get up. If I make a mistake, I will correct it. If I turn away temporarily, I will seek forgiveness and run to Your arms, but I will not deliberately choose a life of failure. I accept my position as a victorious Christian. You have placed me in the winner's circle! Triumph is waiting for me in every situation. It's all found in You!

Simple Truth

No one ever wins a race and declares, "I wish I hadn't run so hard!"

STEADFASTNESS

Be steadfast, immovable,
always excelling in the work of the Lord,
because you know that in the Lord your labor is not in vain.

1 CORINTHIANS 15:58 NRSV

FROM THE FATHER'S HEART

My child, I will develop steadfastness in you as you allow Me to be your employer. Do every job as if you were working for Me—and you will find a new joy and satisfaction. Then you won't be looking for accolades from someone other than Me. Keep your eyes and ears turned heavenward to help you remember your purpose in life and to continue faithfully in the tasks I give you. My applause is all you need.

FROM A SEEKING HEART

Lord, when I see no results, I am tempted to look at the short-term benefits instead of the long-term assignment. My purpose is to know You—not to please others. Although my body and emotions may want to raise a flag of surrender, I will not. I choose the path of steadfastness—not in a get-by mode but always giving You my all, Lord, until my mission and purpose on earth are completed.

SIMPLE TRUTH

When God is our employer, the fringe benefits are out of this world!

YIELDEDNESS

*I consider everything a loss compared to the surpassing
greatness of knowing Christ Jesus my Lord,
for whose sake I have lost all things.*

PHILIPPIANS 3:8

FROM THE FATHER'S HEART

My child, do you value anything in this life more than your
relationship to Me? Are you willing to follow Me at all
costs? Yielding your life to Me means that you are totally
abandoning it for Me to use however I wish. It is not giving
up but giving over—the transference of ownership of your
life to Me. With yieldedness, you can serve Me no matter
what may happen to you or to those around you.

FROM A SEEKING HEART

Lord, without You, what would my life be like? An empty
shell, a meaningless vacuum, a driven individual with a pauper's license for survival! Nothing I own can compare to You,
Lord, and the joy of knowing You intimately. When testing
comes, I know my yieldedness to You will result in even
greater character that You want to produce. Without You, I
am nothing, Lord. My life is Yours; use me as You wish.

SIMPLE TRUTH
Failing to yield is flirting with danger.

OBEDIENCE

Although he was a son,
he learned obedience from what he suffered.

HEBREWS 5:8

FROM THE FATHER'S HEART

My child, do you really, *really* trust Me with your life, even when suffering enters the picture? I am not a harsh dictator; I'm a loving Father who longs for your obedience. When you learn to respect Me as the authority of your life and desire My wants above your own, you will develop obedience. It is trusting Me with the entire contents of your heart, believing that I know what is best for you. I do love you, My child!

FROM A SEEKING HEART

Lord, what a wonderful example of obedience You were! Knowing from the beginning that Your purpose was to die for all sin, You still chose the role of a suffering Savior. I know Your plan for me is perfect and will bring great joy and fulfillment. And I can see by the tracks of my painful disobedience that it's always wise to trust Your leading. I have set my heart on obedience from this point on, Lord. My chief desire is to follow Your wishes and accomplish Your plan—any way You choose for me.

SIMPLE TRUTH

No matter what God asks, just say yes.

AFFECTION

*Be kindly affectioned one to another with brotherly love;
in honour preferring one another.*

ROMANS 12:10 KJV

FROM THE FATHER'S HEART

My child, have My arms ever been too short to hold you? Have I ever withheld My affection from you, even when you disobeyed? Have I not told you, you are the most important creation in My world? Then I want you also to show affection to others by welcoming them into your life with My love. Your affection will give Me freedom to love through you as you make yourself available to Me.

FROM A SEEKING HEART

Father, I could rehearse all the times and places when I have closed the door on others, refusing to show Your love because of busyness or apathy. But I will not go there again. Instead, with repentant heart, I am placing a new welcome mat on the front porch of my heart—one that reaches out with the affection and love of Jesus and says, "Come in! You are welcome here!" Who will You bring to my door today, Lord?

SIMPLE TRUTH

Godly affection changes the complexion of our hearts.

CREATIVITY

*Commit to the LORD whatever you do,
and your plans will succeed.*

PROVERBS 16:3

FROM THE FATHER'S HEART

My child, I have given you the opportunity to participate in My creative process. When you rely on My resources to channel your time and energy into productive outlets, you can enjoy My gift of creativity. You can give Me the freedom to use whatever method I choose to accomplish My purpose in you. You will like the results, and the finished product will bear My stamp of approval.

FROM A SEEKING HEART

Father, being a part of Your creation is a joy in itself, but to share in the work of creating is a privilege. My resources all fall short, but You have unlimited ways of tapping my potential. Lord, how exciting to know that You have special dreams for me and that You are working daily to make them happen. I will use whatever creativity I have to make a difference for You.

SIMPLE TRUTH

Creativity always involves His activity.

NOBILITY

But you are a chosen people, a royal priesthood,
a holy nation, a people belonging to God.

1 PETER 2:9

FROM THE FATHER'S HEART

My child, do you understand that I created you as a unique human being and that you were chosen for My glory and use? Whether you live in a castle or a hovel, you are not a pauper. I am more than able to meet all your needs. Wear My nobility well. Because of My grace, you can respond to My call on your life and choose to live like a child of the King.

FROM A SEEKING HEART

Father, who am I that You would choose to love me as Your own child? Nothing I have done in the past or ever will do can help me inherit Your throne rights. But You paid the price for me to become nobility. I will not waste a day and fail to represent my King. I'll be Your ambassador, Lord. I choose to act with nobility, reverence, and honor to the One I love with all my heart.

SIMPLE TRUTH

It's not where we live but whose we are that makes us the King's kids.

VICTORIOUS SPIRIT

But thanks be to God,
who gives us the victory through our Lord Jesus Christ.

1 CORINTHIANS 15:57 NRSV

FROM THE FATHER'S HEART

My child, I have good news for you. The victory you long
for is available. When you recognize your total freedom in
Christ through His death and resurrection, I will give you a
victorious spirit. You don't need to live in bondage. You can
choose a life of victory by trusting Me to bury all your fears,
your sin, and your failures. Your old life is gone; I have done
a new work in your heart and life!

FROM A SEEKING HEART

Father, forgive me for allowing thoughts of my past failures
and self-condemnation to convince me I could not live with
a victorious spirit. It is what You did, not what I have done,
that gives me victory. By faith I choose to believe You, Lord.
Your Word tells me that victory is mine through what Jesus
did by dying on the cross for me, by crushing death to live
again. Because of Your work, I am dead to sin but alive and
victorious in You.

SIMPLE TRUTH

Just believing isn't enough. It's believing the Truth
that changes lives.

ADVENTURE

By faith Abraham. . .obeyed and went,
even though he did not know where he was going.

HEBREWS 11:8

FROM THE FATHER'S HEART

My child, are you bored with life? I can solve that. Do you long for more adventure in your life? You will find it when you surrender your own fears and preconceived ideas in exchange for the plans I have for you. Whether planned or spontaneous, you can make every moment of your life a joyful and adventurous journey. Are you willing to go whenever and wherever I want you to? Always remember: Sometimes the greatest adventures are under your nose—right where I have already placed you.

FROM A SEEKING HEART

Father, I admit the word *adventure* frightens me at times. Does it mean sending me as an ambassador to a foreign country? Will You call me to a godless place to spend my days in absolute poverty? Yet, Lord, it really doesn't matter. I'm so in love with You that, like Abraham, I want to run out the door the moment You say, "Go!" Whether I go or stay, with or without the full picture, I trust You, Lord. I choose the spirit of adventure, for You are trustworthy and will never lead me astray.

SIMPLE TRUTH
The best ventures are God-adventures.

FRIENDLINESS

Two are better than one,
because they have a good return for their work.

ECCLESIASTES 4:9

FROM THE FATHER'S HEART

My child, when you recognize that other people play a valuable part in your life, you will know something of the value of friendliness. You cannot function well isolated from the benefits others can give you. Trust Me to help you learn from the strengths and weaknesses of others, and make yourself available to help them as well. Those who want friends must make the effort to be friendly.

FROM A SEEKING HEART

Father, You have shown me the value of two. I am tempted to pull away into isolation, wrong thinking, and self-centeredness. But learning from others and realizing how You made us for fellowship opens me up and pulls me out of my temporary shell. There are times to be alone, but, Lord, I will choose to make people a priority like You did, through friendliness.

SIMPLE TRUTH

The road to a friend's house lies somewhere between a
smile and a hug.

PEACE

And the peace of God, which transcends all understanding,
will guard your hearts and your minds in Christ Jesus.

PHILIPPIANS 4:7

FROM THE FATHER'S HEART

My child, there is never a need so great that it should give
you a chicken heart. Don't worry; just pray. My peace is the
knowledge that you are secure in My hands. Allow My
Spirit to pluck out worry and fill you with My presence.
When you surrender your fears and cares to Me, there's no
need to wring your hands and squawk anxiously. I will guard
your heart with calm assurance daily.

FROM A SEEKING HEART

Lord, I refuse to allow fear and worry to make a home in my
heart. Instead, I will submit to You every care and concern,
every need that looms in my mind like a caged animal ready
to spring. In return, I receive from You that blanket of peace
that literally covers me and keeps my enemies from attack-
ing my mind and emotions. In You, I can rest easy and
choose peace.

SIMPLE TRUTH

Nothing is ever out of God's control.

THOUGHTFULNESS

I thank my God every time I remember you.

PHILIPPIANS 1:3

FROM THE FATHER'S HEART

My child, add thoughtfulness to your life by remembering the importance of others as unique creations of Mine. When I develop thoughtfulness in you, you can let others know how valuable they are to Me and to you through a kind word, a tender gesture, or a second-mile gift. You can visualize each day as an opportunity to bring joy into the lives of others. Thoughtfulness does make a difference.

FROM A SEEKING HEART

Lord, just to know You are thinking of me throughout the day—that Your thoughts of me outnumber the grains of sand, makes me know how valuable I am to You. You treated everyone alike, Lord, as valuable creations. I want that kind of thoughtfulness to adorn my character, too. Bring someone into my life today who needs Your thoughtful touch. How can I show Your love to them?

SIMPLE TRUTH

"I-centeredness" brings neglect to the rest of the body.

RESPECTABILITY

A good name is more desirable than great riches;
to be esteemed is better than silver or gold.

PROVERBS 22:1

FROM THE FATHER'S HEART

My child, I love your name. It fits you well. But there is more to your name than the letters your parents chose for you at birth. I will add respectability to that name as you choose to discipline your life according to My Word and ways, so that the name of Christ is always honored. Respectability always seeks to please Me rather than appease people. I never forget your name. Give me the honor of never forgetting Mine.

FROM A SEEKING HEART

Father, there are hundreds of names and attributes that characterize You, and all of them are good. I've lost the desire to make my name known. Instead, Lord, I choose to pursue a reputation that is known for honoring Your name above all names. I choose respectability, Lord, in such a way that when people think of my name, they will also think of Yours.

SIMPLE TRUTH

We are all billboards for something. What does yours advertise?

EXUBERANCE

*"You shall love the LORD your God with all your heart,
and with all your soul, and with all your might."*

DEUTERONOMY 6:5 RSV

FROM THE FATHER'S HEART

My child, I enjoy seeing the exuberance that comes from putting Me first in your life and loving Me with all that you are. Allow Me to implant My desires on the screen of your imagination, so your thoughts and actions are always consumed with love for Me. Examine your heart often, and make sure that nothing or no one tries to replace the love that should be reserved for Me alone. Then get excited about our relationship!

FROM A SEEKING HEART

Lord, when You cry, "Come away, My beloved," my spirit runs to You like a prisoner sprinting for freedom. At times, everything within me cries out, "Abba, Daddy!" as I long for Your strong arms to come and enfold me. Lord, I choose to place all lesser loves at the foot of Your cross. Accept my praise-filled exuberance, Lord; and when no adequate words remain, receive the groanings of a bride in love with her true Lover.

SIMPLE TRUTH

We can never love the Lord too much.

WHOLESOMENESS

A wholesome tongue is a tree of life.

PROVERBS 15:4 KJV

FROM THE FATHER'S HEART

My child, ungodly pursuits and temptations will stalk you like hungry lions hunting their prey. But when you choose to participate in only the things that are helpful and spiritually uplifting in your life, you are developing wholesomeness. Turn away from harmful influences. You can make the decision to let Me speak through you, choosing only those words that will edify and help others.

FROM A SEEKING HEART

Father, if I were training for the Olympics, I would not eat foods that would destroy the growing cells in my body. Neither do I want to feed on tasty morsels of gossip that would destroy my neighbors. And on my computer, I choose antivirus software to protect it against harmful material that could shut down my system. In the same way, I choose wholesomeness, Lord, and give You full freedom to fill my mind with antivirus truths that draw me close to You and help energize others.

SIMPLE TRUTH

Jesus is always the pause that refreshes.

THOROUGHNESS

All Scripture is God-breathed. . .so that the man of God
may be thoroughly equipped for every good work.

2 TIMOTHY 3:16–17

FROM THE FATHER'S HEART

My child, never confuse thoroughness with perfectionism.
Thoroughness exhausts every resource you have in order to
serve Me more effectively. Thoroughness is like excellence.
I will see that each detail of your life is well equipped to accomplish My life's calling for you. When you place your life
and abilities at My disposal, I will enable you to accomplish
otherwise impossible tasks.

FROM A SEEKING HEART

Lord, what a thorough God You are! Down to the most
minute detail—the numbers of hairs on our heads—You
know it all. And the thoroughness of Your plan unfolded
throughout Your Word as everything happened on cue—just
as You foretold. I, too, want thoroughness in my life, leaving
nothing to chance but studying well to make my service to
You not slipshod, but top-shelf. At all times and in all ways,
Lord, You are at work in me, thoroughly filling my spirit and
fueling my efforts.

SIMPLE TRUTH

Halfhearted work produces halfhearted results.

off

REVERENCE

*Therefore, since we are receiving a kingdom
that cannot be shaken, let us be thankful,
and so worship God acceptably with reverence and awe.*

HEBREWS 12:28

FROM THE FATHER'S HEART

My child, when you show reverence, you are humbling yourself in My presence and acknowledging who I really am. While some may believe in man-made religions and self-made successes, your reverence shows Me your genuine character. It is, in reality, recognizing your nothingness in light of My power and greatness. And I, in return, love to lift you up in My presence, for you are My precious child.

FROM A SEEKING HEART

Father, is there anyone who deserves more praise and honor than You? Who but You flung the stars into place and hung the heavens in place? Who but You holds the world together in the palm of Your hand? Lord, I indeed am nothing—and You are everything. Gratitude and awe are what my heart cries when I kneel at Your feet, and reverence is what my heart feels toward You, my Father and my God.

SIMPLE TRUTH

The attitude in which we worship is a good thermometer of our current relationship with God.

CHRISTLIKENESS

Your attitude should be the same as that of Christ Jesus.

PHILIPPIANS 2:5

FROM THE FATHER'S HEART

My child, this is My desire for you—that you grow up to be just like Me. I will develop Christlikeness in you as I pour My love and grace into your life. As a recipient of that love, you will be, like Paul, compelled to act upon that love. How I accomplish this is not your concern. Trust Me, for when you act upon the thoughts and life which I have placed within you, you will bear the characteristics of a Christian. And when you bear My likeness, others will see the fruit of My Spirit firsthand in your life—and you will never be the same again.

FROM A SEEKING HEART

Lord, I still remember the first time I met You. Like a tottering child, I walked with shaky faith and endured many falls. But You have patiently strengthened and painfully taught me that real Christlikeness carries a price tag. The journey is sweet, but, Lord, I have so far to go. Whatever it takes, let me be a mirror that others may see Jesus in me.

SIMPLE TRUTH

When considering the cost of discipleship, remember that some things are priceless.

INDIVIDUALISM

"I have redeemed you;
I have called you by name, you are mine."

ISAIAH 43:1 RSV

FROM THE FATHER'S HEART

My child, you are not a carbon-copy creation. I have given you individualism by creating you as a unique person in Christ. I have taken great care to design unique gifts for you that will enable you to influence others and build up the body of Christ in a special way, unlike any others. No one else can fill your shoes, My child. You are indeed a treasure to Me.

FROM A SEEKING HEART

Father, some of us spend our lives proving that we are no different from anyone else; others devise extravagant schemes to prove they indeed walk to another beat. We are the same in many ways; yet we are created so uniquely. Instead of fighting against my differences, limitations, or weaknesses, Lord, I choose to accept my individualism and use each facet of it as a way to honor You and bless others.

SIMPLE TRUTH

God gives each of us "you-niqueness."

TIRELESSNESS

They will soar on wings like eagles;
they will run and not grow weary,
they will walk and not be faint.

ISAIAH 40:31

FROM THE FATHER'S HEART

My child, when I energize you with My Spirit, I will give you tirelessness—the ability to work on My timetable with a minimum of weariness and a maximum of joy. This will happen as you wait upon Me, trusting that I will give you the strength you need daily—not just to walk and run without weariness but also to soar like the eagle, even against turbulent winds. Aren't you tired of being tired?

FROM A SEEKING HEART

Lord, I recognize my total need for You to take over at all times. These chicken legs falter, and these chicken wings tire of flapping wildly on their own—and accomplishing so little. I am ready to soar, Lord. Give me eagle wings and the fuel of Your Holy Spirit, so that tirelessness will characterize me in Your kingdom's work. I choose to appropriate Your strength daily, Lord!

SIMPLE TRUTH

Chickens may fly for thirteen seconds, but eagles can soar for miles.

HAPPINESS

Happy is he who trusts in the LORD.

PROVERBS 16:20 RSV

FROM THE FATHER'S HEART

My child, will you trust Me daily for every need and circumstance of life? Then you will know happiness. Why? Because happiness won't come through accumulations or successes. Even the poorest can know happiness. It is a choice you can make to lessen your wants and increase your desire for the things of God—regardless of your situation in life. Others will see the difference, and so will you. I am the only One who can ever bring you true happiness.

FROM A SEEKING HEART

Lord, Your upside-down theology challenged people everywhere. Those who were expecting happiness to ride in on the back of a white horse with tax-free benefits couldn't understand. They were anticipating independence, not a dependent trust on You. Lord, I may not understand, either, but I only know You have brought more happiness into my life than I could ever imagine. It's my desire to make every day a carefree, trusting day. I choose happiness, Lord—in You!

SIMPLE TRUTH

Happiness comes from knowing we have nothing—
and yet we have everything in Jesus.

TOLERANCE

Let brotherly love continue.

HEBREWS 13:1 KJV

FROM THE FATHER'S HEART

My child, have you allowed any crusty places to grow in your heart? Are your ears tuned to the right station? Have any clouds blocked your vision? As you refuse to place others in restricted categories of attitude or action and see them through My eyes, I will give you tolerance. You can then dispense love and grace freely, accepting others as unique creations of Mine—not condoning sin but allowing for imperfection and differences of opinion.

FROM A SEEKING HEART

Jesus, when I look at the weaknesses of Your disciples and see how You loved and used them, I know Your tolerance level was high. I can't count the times when You have loved me in spite of my imperfections. Can I do any less for others? It's not my job to mold them into my own image—but to reflect Yours—and to accept others as they are, the way You do. You will do any necessary changing—including changes in me.

SIMPLE TRUTH

If you are the one who is always right and everyone else is wrong—ask the Lord for a second opinion.

INTENTIONALITY

For I delight in your commands because I love them.

PSALM 119:47

FROM THE FATHER'S HEART

My child, you cannot wind your life's time clock and expect it to keep ticking by itself. Choosing indiscriminately will still cause havoc. Intentionality comes when you place such a high value on My priorities for your life that you are willing to do whatever it takes—and whatever I ask—to keep these values important. Set your life by My heart, not by your clock.

FROM A SEEKING HEART

Father, when we allow others to make our choices for us, our priorities suffer. Whether in marriage, in work, in parenting, in school, in church, or at play, Lord, we determine what is most important. Our checkbooks and bodies show it, and our friends and family know it. I want to exercise intentionality, Lord, so that every area of my life lines up with Your priorities. Whatever You value is what I want to value.

SIMPLE TRUTH

Good intentions can fail; but "God intentions" will always succeed.

SENSIBILITY

Do not merely listen to the word, and so deceive yourselves.
Do what it says.

JAMES 1:22

FROM THE FATHER'S HEART

My child, My plans for you are not difficult to discern. But you will need a spiritual hearing aid to apply the truths you hear. I will give you sensibility as you listen carefully to My words of wisdom. Tune your ears once more to My voice, then act quickly upon the things I tell you. Remember that partial obedience is really disobedience.

FROM A SEEKING HEART

Lord, when situations occur that need decisions and when others look to me for wisdom, I need Your sensibility. The Sunday sermons, daily devotionals, and my heart-wrenching searches for the truth will fade if I do not heed what I see in Your mirror and act upon that truth. Lord, I'm listening today a little more closely, and I choose to act with sensibility on the things You say.

SIMPLE TRUTH

From God's viewpoint, sensible does not always mean logical.

PROFESSIONALISM

I will praise you, O Lord my God, with all my heart;
I will glorify your name forever.

PSALM 86:12

FROM THE FATHER'S HEART

My child, it is not how much you do for Me that matters as much as how you do it. I love to see you represent Me in the best way possible with an attitude of excellence. This professionalism is a choice you can make to give Me your all—at all times—to glorify Me and to present Christianity with love and respect. It is a praise garment you wear that will make a difference in My kingdom's work.

FROM A SEEKING HEART

Lord, although You were accused of unprofessional conduct—called a glutton and a winebibber—and ridiculed unmercifully by Your enemies, You always conducted Yourself with professionalism. Never once did You fail to honor and bring glory to Your Father. I need not *feel* like a professional, according to others' meanings, but I can choose to believe my work counts for something. Because every gift and every job is a sacrifice of praise to You, I will act with professionalism and excellence. After all, I serve a King!

SIMPLE TRUTH

Stand tall—and give your all.

HOSPITALITY

*Do not forget to entertain strangers, for by so doing
some people have entertained angels without knowing it.*

HEBREWS 13:2

FROM THE FATHER'S HEART

My child, your willingness to open your heart and home with
Christian friendship, love, and understanding to those who
have spiritual, emotional, or physical needs tells Me you understand the meaning of hospitality. It is recognizing that
everything you are and have belongs to Me and is to be
shared with those whom I bring into your life. Let Me help
you keep your heart and your home open—and I will bless
you in ways you can't imagine.

FROM A SEEKING HEART

Father, fear often hides behind locked doors and closed curtains. But when You walk through our hearts and make
them beautiful places again—places where Your presence
gently warms, places where love truly lives, we can hang a
welcome sign over the door with great enthusiasm. Remove
whatever barriers keep me from hospitality, Lord, and may
Your heart and others always feel welcome here.

SIMPLE TRUTH

*A feast is nice to feed a few—but a cup of cold water
will also do.*

OUTSPOKENNESS

Let the redeemed of the LORD say so.

PSALM 107:2 KJV

FROM THE FATHER'S HEART

My child, always think and pray before you speak. Remember that outspokenness is good when it is the compelling desire to let others around you know about Me. Because of My goodness to you and the power I give to you, you can boldly and confidently share the good news of Jesus' love with others. I will loosen your tongue and warm your heart so My love can radiate through you.

FROM A SEEKING HEART

Father, I am so quick to say, "Guess what?" when special surprises or blessings arrive on my doorstep. May I be just as prompt to speak out the good news of Jesus to those around me. I choose outspokenness—only in the desire that my words might be "apples of gold in pictures of silver" to those who need Your love, Your comfort, and Your life-giving purpose. Lord, I bless You today!

SIMPLE TRUTH

Telling is compelling when we truly know the Lord.

CONSISTENCY

Be prepared in season and out of season.

2 TIMOTHY 4:2

FROM THE FATHER'S HEART

My child, I will give you consistency as you keep your eyes fixed on Me. No matter what your emotions dictate, remember they are like harmless, yapping dogs trying to attack your devotion. Your emotions are unreliable and will change, but I never change. I will help you keep your testimony fun and secure. Choose to make yourself available to Me, and allow Me to use you in any situation.

FROM A SEEKING HEART

Lord, Your rock-solid consistency challenges me to keep on, even when everything and everyone around me says, "Quit!" I choose by faith to walk daily close to Your side, establishing habits that will breed faithfulness and consistency. I will prepare myself by feeding on Your Word so that the Holy Spirit can turn ordinary encounters into divine opportunities.

SIMPLE TRUTH

Keep on keeping on. . .and on. . .and on.

SEPARATENESS

"Therefore come out from them and be separate, says the Lord."

2 CORINTHIANS 6:17

FROM THE FATHER'S HEART

My child, when you answer My call to discipleship, you accept the role of separateness, too. Separateness is the willingness to walk alone if necessary to better accomplish My purposes. Others may choose empty pursuits and vain pleasures, but you cannot. I do not ask you to remove yourself from the world—only to be light in a dark world for Me.

FROM A SEEKING HEART

Lord, at times I've rebelled, snared in the clutches of conformity. "Different" was not my choice—I only wanted to be like everyone else. But Your calling woos me continuously to the incredible privilege of separateness—not a boastful, pharisaical, "be like me" attitude; rather it's an intense longing that cries out, "Be like Jesus!" Your example motivates me: always fitting in, yet always standing out. You humbly walked alone, all the time drawing people into the holiness of heaven.

SIMPLE TRUTH

Standing out often means standing up—even when no one else does.

FAIRNESS

"For in the same way you judge others, you will be judged,
and with the measure you use, it will be measured to you."

MATTHEW 7:2

FROM THE FATHER'S HEART

My child, I have created all people equally, and I love them all the same. But not all will love Me the same. Not everyone will treat you fairly, either. However, you can exercise fairness by recognizing the limitations of others and treating them the same way you want Me to treat you. Fairness is respecting the freedom of others without forcing your convictions on them.

FROM A SEEKING HEART

Father, often my expectations of others are exceeded only by my expectations of myself. When I do this, I'm setting myself and others up for failure in my own eyes. Let me instead see others as You see them and give allowance for mistakes—and growth. I have no right to dictate my standards to others but every right to share what Your expectations are. Lord, today help me model fairness to my fellow brothers and sisters.

SIMPLE TRUTH

What is right may not always seem like what is fair.

DILIGENCE

Be diligent that ye may be found of him in peace,
without spot, and blameless.

2 PETER 3:14 KJV

FROM THE FATHER'S HEART

My child, life is hard, but I am here, and I am your strength. Never assume that your work is unimportant. Diligence comes when you recognize the value of each responsibility I give, whether large or small, and when you determine to work through a problem, task, or assignment without giving up. If you will let them, the very difficulties I allow into your life will drive you toward Me and make you more Christlike.

FROM A SEEKING HEART

Lord, I look at Your life and work, and my small contribution seems so insignificant. Thank You for reminding me daily that You value me and expect me to multiply what You have given me—daily pressing on to reach the potential You have designed for my life. My eyes and my heart are fixed on You. When problems perplex me, I will seek Your help. I desire to work faithfully with diligence, Lord.

SIMPLE TRUTH

It is not how much we do but how well we do it that matters.

ORDERLINESS

But everything should be done in a fitting and orderly way.

1 CORINTHIANS 14:40

FROM THE FATHER'S HEART

My child, have you been clinging to excuses again? Remember, undisciplined lives are like cities with broken-down walls. You will give your enemy free entrance to take control if you do not repair the walls. You can develop orderliness by establishing restraint and good habits in your life. As you allow Me to remove the clutter, I will show you the disciplines necessary to rebuild and keep your life under My Spirit's control.

FROM A SEEKING HEART

Father, from a human standpoint, I'm grateful that orderliness does not always equate organization! However, as I look at Your world, I see how every creation—large or small—fits Your perfect plan. You knew what You were doing! We, on the other hand, have cluttered Your creation with the debris of undisciplined lives. Lord, You have my permission—I invite You—to clean my house often, so orderliness may characterize anything I do. I choose not compulsive, white-washed hands but submission—a total cleaning of the heart.

SIMPLE TRUTH

It is the cleanliness of the heart that is next to godliness.

SECURITY

Set your minds on things above, not on earthly things.

COLOSSIANS 3:2

FROM THE FATHER'S HEART

My child, have you learned that I am the only security you need? All other promises are like empty balloons blown away by the first gust of wind. Real security comes when you place your thoughts on eternal things rather than temporal. As you set your heart on Me, I will fill you with a hope that endures and a peace that passes all understanding.

FROM A SEEKING HEART

Father, forgive me for the times I've looked to other sources for the security in my life. These lesser pursuits promise much but deliver little. Only You, Lord, can bring lasting security. When I am tempted to set my heart on earthly treasures and values, I will remember Your words of truth. I choose You, Lord, and the eternal peace and security You give when we place our trust in You.

SIMPLE TRUTH

Maturity understands the meaning of real security.

RADIANCE

*The path of the righteous is like the first gleam of dawn,
shining ever brighter till the full light of day.*

PROVERBS 4:18

FROM THE FATHER'S HEART

My child, what do others see when they look in your face?
Is there a glow about your countenance like My servants
Moses and Stephen? I will give you radiance as you look
into My face and mirror My love. I will help you make your
life a reflection of Mine so that others can see Jesus shining
through you. That light will shine because of an inner fuel,
not because of any outward adornment.

FROM A SEEKING HEART

Lord, You were such a beautiful reflection of Your heavenly
Father. Anyone who looked at You saw what God was like. I
long to let Your radiance shine through me, Lord, and to let
the transparent glow of a transformed life lead others to You.
I desire to live in Your presence daily—to live so close to You
that Your light will grow brighter every day—so close that others will know I have been with You, and they will glorify You.

SIMPLE TRUTH

*We do not become mirrors by adding external reflectors
but by living daily in His light.*

BUOYANCY

*I had fainted, unless I had believed to see the goodness
of the LORD in the land of the living.*

PSALM 27:13 KJV

FROM THE FATHER'S HEART

My child, do you feel sometimes as if you cannot swim another stroke? I will never abandon you. I am here to give you buoyancy—the ability to stay afloat in the midst of drowning circumstances. I will enable you to hang on and bounce back after adversity. When you trust Me to be your Lighthouse, you will find safe shores again.

FROM A SEEKING HEART

Father, I remember the times You reached out Your hand to pull me into Your lifeboat when I was sinking. But other days You seemed to disappear. In those moments, Lord, You've taught me to keep on trusting and assured me that the Light is in sight. I recognize buoyancy is something I need daily. You have given me every reason to trust Your faithfulness. With Your help, I can tread water as long as You require, because I believe in Your total goodness and plan for my life.

SIMPLE TRUTH

*Through Christ we can hold on—even when no hope
is in sight.*

UNDERSTANDING

Wise conduct is pleasure to a man of understanding.

PROVERBS 10:23 RSV

FROM THE FATHER'S HEART

My child, when you gain understanding, you become aware of My power and wisdom. I will give you the ability to channel your mind in positive, wise directions, so you can receive clear messages from My Word. Then your actions will verify your beliefs, and My name will be honored. Always follow My ways and look to Me for understanding.

FROM A SEEKING HEART

Father, how I want to understand Your truths! How can I possibly teach others if I have no understanding myself? I search for treasures in Your Word like nuggets of gold. Words I have read hundreds of times before suddenly take on new meaning, and truth floods in; understanding follows. Yet there is so much more I want to know about You. Keep teaching me, Lord. I choose to find understanding so I can then live out those truths daily.

SIMPLE TRUTH

Some things will remain a surprise until eternity.

Day 122

ATTRACTIVENESS

*Show that they can be fully trusted, so that in every way they
will make the teaching about God our Savior attractive.*

TITUS 2:10

FROM THE FATHER'S HEART

My child, I do want you to look your best at all times, but
your physical appearance is not nearly as important as your
inner character. I see attractiveness in you when you let Me
adorn your heart and spirit with Christlikeness. When you
choose the wardrobe of My righteousness, the garment of
praise, and the spirit of loveliness, others will be attracted to
the "Jesus" in you.

FROM A SEEKING HEART

Father, You are the real beautician of my life. Expensive
wardrobes, trendy hairstyles—not even cosmetic surgery
can make me beautiful inside. The kind of attractiveness I
choose, Lord, is the complete makeover of Your Spirit on
my inner life. Redo my heart; renew my spirit, so my beauty
will be soul deep. The goal is not to draw people to me but
to attract them to the One who can change their lives. Lord,
change even my countenance to reflect You.

SIMPLE TRUTH
   *Reflections are never distorted when we look to God
   for the truth.*

ADMIRATION

"Stop and consider God's wonders."

JOB 37:14

FROM THE FATHER'S HEART

My child, I see admiration in you when you revere Me for who I am. Many applaud Me because of what I can do for them, but I love the heart that offers pure praise as a sacrifice. It says to Me that you recognize your own limitations and that you love to celebrate Me with awesome wonder and a desire to pattern your life after Mine.

FROM A SEEKING HEART

Lord, have I told You lately that You are my hero? You are truly the reason for any good thing that springs up in me. When I "grow up," I want to be just like You, Jesus. I choose to revere You and to develop that quality of admiration, so that I will never forget my roots—where I came from and where I am going. There is no one like You!

SIMPLE TRUTH

To the Lord, fearing Him means revering Him.

SHARPNESS

The unfolding of your words gives light;
it gives understanding to the simple.

PSALM 119:130

FROM THE FATHER'S HEART

My child, what have you been listening to lately? Don't be like those who are dull in hearing, for they have sedated their hearts and shut out My voice. I will give sharpness as you listen attentively to My words. When you turn your eyes and ears toward Me, I will fill you with light and an eagerness to learn even more. Even the simple will understand My truth if they really listen.

FROM A SEEKING HEART

Father, in the dark areas of my heart, You shine Your light, and understanding floods my thoughts. My mind cannot conceive and my life can never achieve all the things You have planned for me to know and do without Your supernatural intervention. There is a hunger in my heart to know, to understand, to experience You and all of Your fullness, Lord. Father, grant me sharpness so I can always be on the cutting edge of Your work.

SIMPLE TRUTH
Dull the mind—and you darken the heart.

CREDIBILITY

He that abideth in me, and I in him, the same bringeth forth much fruit: for without me ye can do nothing.

JOHN 15:5 KJV

FROM THE FATHER'S HEART

My child, with ownership comes responsibility. Credibility recognizes that My cause could be hindered or edified by your actions and beliefs. As you abide in Me, I will abide in you. I want to produce much fruit in your life—much more than you can ever envision. Knowing that others are watching your life should create a greater desire to let Me be glorified in you.

FROM A SEEKING HEART

Lord, many refused to acknowledge You and to believe You were really the Son of God, but You never lost Your credibility. Every word, every motive, every thought reflected the authority and character of Your heavenly Father. Help me realize that credibility is a choice I can make daily to let my life do the talking. May everything in me and about me glorify You, Lord, and cause others to believe You are the Way, the Truth, and the Life.

SIMPLE TRUTH
Credibility is our ability to stay tuned to God.

FAITH

*"If you have faith as small as a mustard seed. . .
nothing will be impossible for you."*

MATTHEW 17:20

FROM THE FATHER'S HEART

My child, I give each of My children a seed of faith. Then
you must decide how to grow it. Growth will come when
you give Me the freedom to work out the details of your
life—past, present, and future—in a way that will honor Me
the most. Trust Me with every circumstance, and believe
that nothing is impossible with Me. There are mountains
just waiting to be moved.

FROM A SEEKING HEART

Father, my faith needs ample supplies of Your fertilizing Word
and daily drinks from Your Living Water. Walking through
the valley, emerging from the mud, and bathing again in Your
sweet springs of mercy have taught me I can indeed trust
Your faithfulness. Truly, when I couldn't see a way out, You
brought me through it. When I remember Your track record, how can I choose anything else during difficult times?
Rather than doubt, I choose to faith it out!

SIMPLE TRUTH

*When we don't know what to do, faith in God will
see us through.*

RESOURCEFULNESS

"The Holy Spirit, whom the Father will send in my name, will teach you all things and will remind you of everything I have said to you."

JOHN 14:26

FROM THE FATHER'S HEART

My child, you are never alone in your assignment. I have given all My children work to do. But resourcefulness is using the gifts I have given you, along with many others, to broaden the kingdom of God. Take time to look around you, and pray about the laborers—and the gifts needed for each task. Remember, nothing is impossible.

FROM A SEEKING HEART

Father, when I see the needs around me and the work still to be done, it's easy to shy away from responsibility and make excuses. But knowing You have already provided everything I need reminds me that faith is required. When knowledge is lacking, Your Spirit will teach me, and when workers are lacking, You will send them. You are constantly "enlarging my territory." Lord, I will use wisely the resourcefulness You have given me to make Your name known and to accomplish the work You have given me.

SIMPLE TRUTH

If it's going to be—it's up to Thee.

GOODNESS

*For the fruit of the Spirit is in all goodness
and righteousness and truth.*

EPHESIANS 5:9 KJV

FROM THE FATHER'S HEART

My child, when My Spirit produces goodness in you, what a blessing you are to others! That goodness includes the security of knowing you are Mine. It means that because of My love for you, you can turn your thoughts away from yourself and lavish that same kind of love on others with no thought of a return investment. Then you will truly understand something of My work as I went about "doing good."

FROM A SEEKING HEART

Lord, when there is nothing good in me, how can I mirror Your goodness? Only as You manifest Your goodness through my life will that happen. You delighted in oiling squeaky lives, restoring broken dreams, feeding hungry hearts, and even blessing little children. Nothing about You demanded a king's treatment; yet You were God in the flesh. Opportunities to do good lie all around me. Lord, let goodness flow from my life like a bubbling fountain, splashing others with living water.

SIMPLE TRUTH

Goodness stems from love; "shouldness" comes from duty.

FIDELITY

Now it is required that those who have been given a trust must prove faithful.

1 CORINTHIANS 4:2

FROM THE FATHER'S HEART

My child, the more I give to you, the more I expect you to be faithful. You will learn fidelity as you make certain you follow through with every promise, every task, and every intention I lay on your heart. I have trusted you with My work. Will you trust Me with your life? With My help you can become a promise keeper, not a promise breaker.

FROM A SEEKING HEART

Father, I will not dig a hole and bury my talents. And I will not make excuses for any slothfulness. What You are asking of me, what You want to give me—fidelity—is a privilege that I do not want to take lightly. Should I fail, I will take responsibility for my own actions—but I will run back to You quickly. Lord, I want to wear fidelity around my neck. Today I choose to trust You—and to be trusted. I want fidelity, Lord.

SIMPLE TRUTH

God's promise is more than a promise. It is an unchanging fact.

MOBILITY

I will instruct you and teach you in the way you should go.

PSALM 32:8

FROM THE FATHER'S HEART

My child, you do not need a daily road map, other than My Word, to shine light on your journey. All you need is the willingness to trust Me for each day's steps. That willingness is mobility—agreeing to go wherever I lead you, looking ahead, not behind. It is trusting Me even in paths you do not understand and giving Me freedom to change direction if necessary.

FROM A SEEKING HEART

Lord, I see Your mobility in Your Word and throughout Your ministry. You called no place "home" except Your Father's house in heaven. You traveled daily where Your Father sent You. In every way You fulfilled the plans Your Father's fingers had drawn. Like Noah, like Moses, like scores of Your servants—and most of all, like You, Lord—I choose to plant my roots firmly in the Father's heart, not in any earthly foundation. I choose mobility—to follow wherever You decide for me to go.

SIMPLE TRUTH
With each step of faith comes another shimmer of light.

LIVELINESS

" 'Would that you were cold or hot!' "

REVELATION 3:15 RSV

FROM THE FATHER'S HEART

My child, who wants to mirror a graveyard countenance? And who likes drinking from a lukewarm mountain stream? What I want for you is liveliness—an attitude of excitement and warmth toward spiritual things. You can draw vitality and strength from Me so that I can use you and remove any deadness from your life. Then you will truly be like a tree planted by rivers of water—alive and green!

FROM A SEEKING HEART

Father, when my eyes awake every morning, I cry out of thirst for more of You. When darkness falls and day is done, my prayer to You is, "Keep filling me, Lord, with more of You!" But throughout the day, challenges come to drain my strength and lull me into a bed of complacency. God, as Your children, we are so needy! Even if it means firing up the oven so I feel the heat, Lord, don't let me fall into an uncaring, cold mentality. Liveliness is something I want all day long— always crying for more of You, Lord, more of You!

SIMPLE TRUTH

I once was blind, but now I see; I once was dead— now Christ lives in me!

WARINESS

Therefore let us not sleep, as do others;
but let us watch and be sober.

1 THESSALONIANS 5:6 KJV

FROM THE FATHER'S HEART

My child, you cannot afford to let complacency take root in your heart. Instead, let Me develop a spirit of wariness in you—a choice to keep your eyes on Me, especially when things are turbulent around you. Prepare yourself for battle by exercising self-discipline and maintaining an attitude of caution. Your enemy wants to destroy you. But with My power, you will be ready for anything.

FROM A SEEKING HEART

Father, danger faces me constantly, and I cannot depend on others to step in and fight my battles for me. The choices I make daily—to ask for guidance and wisdom, to meditate on Your Word, and to select carefully the influences I let into my mind will help me keep wariness in my life. Lord, I'm keeping my eyes on You.

SIMPLE TRUTH

The enemy loves to catch his victims sleeping.

CONTENTMENT

I have learned to be content whatever the circumstances.

PHILIPPIANS 4:11

FROM THE FATHER'S HEART

My child, you will know something of contentment when you learn to value the simple things of life more than success, riches, or fame. Why strive for treasures that never last and for pleasures that soon are past? Instead, rest in My daily provision and in My control of your circumstances. Contentment brings freedom to enjoy the best things I have planned for you.

FROM A SEEKING HEART

Lord, You were a model of contentment—never complaining and always trusting Your heavenly Father for every provision. You had no home, no income, no luxuries—just the clothes on Your back, the daily bread from Your Father, the hospitality of friends, and a three-year mission that would change the world. I need so little; yet my wants grow foolishly when I'm caught off guard. I want to rest in You, Lord. Let the first words I offer You daily be, "Thank You, Lord. I find contentment in You alone."

SIMPLE TRUTH
We need no stuff. Jesus is enough.

CAUTION

Be self-controlled and alert. Your enemy the devil prowls
around like a roaring lion looking for someone to devour.

1 PETER 5:8

FROM THE FATHER'S HEART

My child, open your eyes and heed My warnings. If you
stand too close to a flame, it will burn you. Learn caution by
recognizing the potential danger in even seemingly harmless situations. Let your spirit be driven and controlled by
Me, and nurture a strong desire for good to prevail. Your
enemy would love to destroy you and your reputation. But
My Spirit is always with you to bring victory and wisdom.

FROM A SEEKING HEART

Father, just to have innocent motives is not enough in the
face of deadly enemies. Grant me wisdom to choose wisely,
discernment to recognize the truth, but most of all, help me
to exercise caution wherever I go. You have given me freedom through Christ, but I refuse to use it foolishly or stub-
bornly, thinking I know better. Lord, I am helpless without
You! I choose caution, Lord, and invite You to go before me
and search out the danger.

SIMPLE TRUTH

It's easier to say no than to attempt lion taming.

PURITY

Blessed are the pure in heart: for they shall see God.

MATTHEW 5:8 KJV

FROM THE FATHER'S HEART

My child, have you ever tried to see your reflection in a dirty mirror? Those who are pure in heart have allowed Me to bathe them with My Holy Spirit until their hearts are clean before Me. Purity keeps your heart and life clean as a vessel of honor so you can see Me clearly, and I can be reflected in you.

FROM A SEEKING HEART

Father, only You can wash away the stains of sin and make us clean again. Only You can bring pure water from a dirty fountain. Only You can place the desire in our hearts to stay pure and holy for You. Make me that kind of vessel, Lord. I long to be a beautiful reflection of Your character. Regardless of the temptation, Your example of purity drives me toward You.

SIMPLE TRUTH

Can others say about us: "Like Father, like son or daughter"?

INSIGHT

*And this is my prayer: that your love may abound more
and more in knowledge and depth of insight.*

PHILIPPIANS 1:9

FROM THE FATHER'S HEART

My child, would you like for the Scriptures to burn in your
heart as you read My Word? Would you like to know more
of My secrets? I will give you insight when you let My
words and My will permeate your spirit. Shut out all other
voices. As you listen to Me speak through My Word, I will
help you understand more of My heart and more of My
great love for you.

FROM A SEEKING HEART

Father, sometimes Your Word whispers gentle reminders to
me about Your character and Your love. Other times Your
Word jolts my spirit like thunderbolts, illuminating my heart
with amazing insight. Each time I seek You, You are faithful
to meet me and open my eyes to know more of You. And,
Lord, the more I know of You, the more I want to know. Give
me Your insight, Lord, not for my own pleasure, but so I can
wrap these truths and present them as healing gifts to others.

SIMPLE TRUTH

We cannot share what we do not know.

OUTREACH

*Each of you should look not only to your own interests,
but also to the interests of others.*

PHILIPPIANS 2:4

FROM THE FATHER'S HEART

My child, remember that I died not only for you; I died for
the whole world. I want your hands, your eyes, your feet,
your heart, and your mouth to convey My love to others
who don't know about Me. I will give you a spirit of out-
reach as you turn your eyes away from yourself to others.
Because I have reached out to you, you can minister to the
emotional, spiritual, and physical needs of others.

FROM A SEEKING HEART

Lord, I love to sit at Your table feasting on the good things
You provide. Your sweet manna is so. . .heavenly! But You did
not call me to count up Your blessings and hoard them daily.
I want to pass them on to others. Forgive me when I become
self-absorbed or uncaring. Lord, I truly want to reach out and
touch others with the same love You give to me.

SIMPLE TRUTH

Hands were made to reach outward, not inward.

FRANKNESS

A rebuke goes deeper into a man of understanding.

PROVERBS 17:10 RSV

FROM THE FATHER'S HEART

My child, all My children need accountability. When you see one of them stray, I want you to learn to use frankness lovingly—caring enough to confront another in order to bring about truth and restoration. With My help, you can pray carefully and seek My wisdom before you speak, making sure your life is right and that My spirit is doing the correction, not you. Speak the truth gently and with love. A fool will reject you, but a wise person will receive My words gratefully. Just obey, and leave the results to Me.

FROM A SEEKING HEART

Lord, of the many responsibilities You ask from Your children, frankness is one of the hardest. Oh, not to blurt out the truth. But to confront in love and to make sure we are not finger-pointing in an area where we, too, are weak—this is our dilemma. However, I will listen for Your voice, seek Your face, and look to Your Word for the help I need when You ask me to confront. Lord, keep me pure in heart, and let frankness be something that is done lovingly and effectively.

SIMPLE TRUTH

Frankness is not an excuse to vent our own displeasure.

SUCCESS

"Do not let this Book of the Law depart from your mouth;
meditate on it day and night. . . .
Then you will be prosperous and successful."

JOSHUA 1:8

FROM THE FATHER'S HEART

My child, may I tell you what success means to Me? It's not how high you build your dreams but how high your faith can climb. It's not how many goals you reach but how many lives you let Me touch through you. Success comes when you value the things in My kingdom more than any earthly treasures. It is saturating yourself with My Word so much that obedience becomes a natural response for you. I will make you successful if you will let Me.

FROM A SEEKING HEART

Lord, once again I look to You as my model for success. I've tried on my own to make a difference. Straining for accomplishments that fade with time, copying others to find my place, and hiding behind a facade of excuses when I failed never materialized into anything worthwhile. Real success comes from knowing You and from letting Your Word take root in my heart so that it can spring up with fruits of the Spirit from You. Lord, I choose Your kind of success.

SIMPLE TRUTH

Those who climb ladders recklessly set themselves up
for falling.

HOPEFULNESS

In his great mercy he has given us new birth into a living hope
through the resurrection of Jesus Christ from the dead.

1 PETER 1:3

FROM THE FATHER'S HEART

My child, you can learn a powerful lesson from the sorrows
and difficulties you experience here on earth. Would you
yearn for heaven, your real home, if everything were perfect
here? I want you to experience real hopefulness—living
joyfully in the new freedom in Christ I have given you.
Hopefulness is basing your life on your future destiny with
Me rather than tying yourself too closely to the events that
happen on earth.

FROM A SEEKING HEART

Lord, if You had not risen from the dead, we would experience no hope—no joy in our hearts, no purpose in life, no
victory over sin, and no real home in heaven. How grateful
I am for Your death and resurrection! Because of Your great
mercy, I choose to live in hopefulness, not despair. When
others ask why, without hesitation I can point to the cross
and say victoriously, "Because of Jesus!"

SIMPLE TRUTH

Only the dead in Christ can truly rise in joy.

URGENCY

"We must work the works of him who sent me,
while it is day; night comes, when no one can work."

JOHN 9:4 RSV

FROM THE FATHER'S HEART

My child, I have appointed the days of your life, and they will pass quicker than you think. I have given you a special task to do while you live on this earth. You can pass the days in wasteful, meaningless activity, or you can use your time and energy wisely, realizing that life is short and that I am coming soon. I need you to choose a sense of urgency. The time is coming when all work will cease—and it will be too late.

FROM A SEEKING HEART

Lord, there is so much I want to do for You and be for You. At times I am easily distracted; yet my heart longs to make every day count as if it were my last. My neighbor may not have tomorrow; I may not even have today; and You may return any moment. Truly teach me to number my days, Lord, that I might present You with a life well lived, radically obedient and emptied of self for You. Keep that sense of urgency in my spirit.

SIMPLE TRUTH

Now is the only time we can count on.

PERSEVERANCE

To that end keep alert with all perseverance,
making supplication for all the saints.

EPHESIANS 6:18 RSV

FROM THE FATHER'S HEART

My child, quitters never win. Keep seeking My heart, and I will develop perseverance in you—the determination to keep on obeying and doing right no matter what happens. Your enemies are relentless, and you must stay alert at all times. Whether in prayer, in personal battles, or in defense of righteousness and justice, you can remain true and faithful with My help.

FROM A SEEKING HEART

Lord, for three years You persevered in the task Your Father assigned You. Never once did You abandon His will for Your life. Just like Your disciples, Lord, I have failed You many times. Yet You never abandoned them, either. You just kept working in their lives, helping them persevere until their missions were completed. Lord, I choose perseverance, too. Hold me up so I will not let You down, until I, too, have finished Your plan for my life.

SIMPLE TRUTH

Anything worth doing is worth doing for the Lord.

CONSTANCY

Blessed are they who maintain justice,
who constantly do what is right.

Psalm 106:3

From the Father's Heart

My child, are you willing to stand up for Me at all costs? If so, I will give you constancy and help you to be strong and unchanging, even when it would be easier to give in and give up. Trust Me that whatever I send your way will not be more than you can handle. I will give you the strength to face anything.

From a Seeking Heart

Father, in this changing world, there is no one who is constant and unchanging but You. How I need You to combat my fickleness in the face of difficulty! I've been on the edge, almost surrendering in defeat. But then You drew me close again and whispered sweet promises in my ear. Your Spirit reminds me daily that I can choose constancy.

Simple Truth

When you get to the end of your life, will you be able
to look back and say, "I did it His way"?

CAREFULNESS

I want you to stress these things,
so that those who have trusted in God may be careful
to devote themselves to doing what is good.
These things are excellent and profitable for everyone.

TITUS 3:8

FROM THE FATHER'S HEART

My child, you face many good choices every day. But watch for ways to show excellence. Make sure your heart is a clean reflector. I will help you learn carefulness, living transparently so that My character can be reflected in your actions and expressions. Always keep your eyes and ears open to My Spirit, listening and watching for My instructions. You can never go wrong doing what is good.

FROM A SEEKING HEART

Father, make me a student of Yours whose classes are never out. Help me study carefully Your ways, Your character, and Your Word, so I can not only learn to know You more intimately but to teach others as well. I will act with carefulness, moving only at Your command and watching for ways You will help me make an eternal difference in the lives of others.

SIMPLE TRUTH

Good doers are far more effective than do-gooders.

DEVOTION

Devote yourselves to prayer, being watchful and thankful.

COLOSSIANS 4:2

FROM THE FATHER'S HEART

My child, I need your devotion—choosing allegiance to Me and opposing anything that might interfere with your faith or convictions. True devotion will make you value My companionship more than any other relationship, and it will keep you cultivating an attitude of reverence and thanksgiving to Me. In a nutshell, I want you to be—simply devoted to Me.

FROM A SEEKING HEART

Lord, Your devotion to Your heavenly Father shone in a multitude of ways: always following His will, always giving Him credit, but most of all, constantly spending time with Him in prayer. Lord, at Your feet is where I can pour out my heart in brokenness and gratitude. On my knees is where I find forgiveness and restored faith. And through constant prayer, I can hear Your heartbeat for the world. Lord, may my devotion always be to You—and to You only.

SIMPLE TRUTH

In a world of constant commotion, choose a life of sweet devotion.

EARNESTNESS

O God, you are my God, earnestly I seek you;
my soul thirsts for you, my body longs for you.

PSALM 63:1

FROM THE FATHER'S HEART

My child, do you remember what it was like when your throat
was parched from fever or extremely hot temperature? All you
wanted then was a long, cool drink of refreshing water—
something to quench your thirst. That's how I want you to feel
about Me. When you express a strong desire to pursue Me
and to know Me deeply, you know something of earnestness.
As you seek Me with a hungry heart and submissive life, I will
satisfy your longings and quench your thirst.

FROM A SEEKING HEART

Father, I have tried to satisfy my hunger and thirst with tasty
morsels and quick sips of earthly pleasures. But they only leave
me parched and wanting more—for something that will last.
When I found You, I knew I had found my true Love. Only
You can fill the hunger left by sin's scars. Only You can satisfy
a spirit shriveled through weariness and disappointment. Like
the psalmist, I, too, long for You, Lord. Let earnestness drive
me to You, Lord. Only there will I be content.

SIMPLE TRUTH

Jesus is the only thirst-quencher.

RESISTANCE

Resist the devil, and he will flee from you.

JAMES 4:7 KJV

FROM THE FATHER'S HEART

My child, have you had your "shots" lately? You will develop resistance by letting Me inoculate you with My Word and My presence so that you can withstand the pressure of anti-Christian influences. It's not a matter of *whether* opposition may come but *when* it will come. You can choose to hide My Word in your heart to help you prepare your life for inevitable battle.

FROM A SEEKING HEART

Father, when I was anemic with sin, You gave me a "blood" transfusion by dying for me, forgiving me, and covering me with Your goodness when I had none of my own. I am not afraid of the convicting needles of Your Spirit, Lord. Point out the areas where I am weak, and daily I will build up the quality of resistance with Your help. Only in You am I strong enough to resist the enemy.

SIMPLE TRUTH

One shot of Truth daily can protect us from even the worst lies.

GRACE

For it is by grace you have been saved, through faith.

EPHESIANS 2:8

FROM THE FATHER'S HEART

My child, turn loose of the past. The moment you asked, your sins were forgiven. I have given you grace as I have erased your mistakes and failures and covered them with My love. When you accept My love, I empower you to exercise the same grace to overlook the faults of others also and to accept them as they are in Christ. Grace never excuses sin but offers undeserved pardon and acceptance as a gift.

FROM A SEEKING HEART

Lord, thank You for this wonderful gift of grace. When I was steeped in the poverty of sin, You held out a silver platter of grace to me and welcomed me into Your family. In You I found a wealth of love, mercy, and forgiveness. Because of Your gift to me, I want grace to characterize my life, Lord. When a brother or sister falls or errs along the way, let my hand be the one that reaches out and pulls them into Your fold. I will shower others with the same undeserved grace You gave to me.

SIMPLE TRUTH

Grace can carve a loving place into even the hardest of hearts.

WIT

There is a time for everything. . . .
A time to weep and a time to laugh. . .

ECCLESIASTES 3:1, 4

FROM THE FATHER'S HEART

My child, I did not create you to walk somberly but soberly.
There is a time for everything. One of the qualities I want
to develop in you is wit—a gift that enables you to lighten
the lives of others with humor and laughter. It's not foolish
mirth; it's learning to celebrate life with joy and spontaneity,
refusing to take circumstances or the differences you have
with others too personally.

FROM A SEEKING HEART

Father, life is too short to frown our way through. When others express opposite opinions and see things differently than
me, I will not be offended. And if someone substitutes another plan for mine, I will let the spontaneity of the moment
interrupt my seriousness. I choose to listen and learn from
You and others, lighten up my own personality, and allow wit
and laughter to brighten the lives of others. For life, after all,
is about celebrating the joy of knowing You.

SIMPLE TRUTH

Laughter can lighten the heaviest of hearts.

DECENCY

Dress modestly, with decency and propriety.

1 TIMOTHY 2:9

FROM THE FATHER'S HEART

My child, remember that wherever you go, you are an ambassador for My kingdom. A prince and princess do not act or dress to please themselves. They make sure everything about them honors their royal family. When you choose decency, you are letting Me dictate the standards of your life, honoring Me with your thoughts, your actions, and even your appearance. In this way, you are showing consideration for others and for the One you represent.

FROM A SEEKING HEART

Lord, I choose to have no standards but Yours. I want every thought, every motive, every deed, and every article of clothing I wear to say "Christian." I can rebel, claiming that freedom in Christ allows me individualism. And that's true, except I refuse to use that freedom selfishly. Why would I want to dishonor the One who gave His all for me and who died for me? Decency makes me want to call attention not to myself but to You, Lord.

SIMPLE TRUTH

Decency makes me care—even about what I wear.

COURAGE

For God hath not given us the spirit of fear;
but of power, and of love, and of a sound mind.

2 TIMOTHY 1:7 KJV

FROM THE FATHER'S HEART

My child, whenever you feel fear creeping into your mind, you can know that that fear is not from Me but from your enemy. Your convictions will be tested, and your faith will be sifted in times of difficulty. I want to fill you with courage—the ability to determine what is valued. I will help you to reach beyond yourself to a strength that is greater than your own, and you'll be willing to stand with Me with a faith that is greater than fear.

FROM A SEEKING HEART

Lord, because of You, these goose bumps of fear have turned into porcupine needles of courage. No longer will I be tossed back and forth with indecisiveness and timidity. You have given me courage to stand tall, hold my shoulders back, and face my enemies head-on. Because I know You are always with me and because You have given me a spirit of power and love, not fear, I can choose to act courageously with conviction and faith.

SIMPLE TRUTH

Courage begins with the first step.

SIMPLICITY

He that giveth, let him do it with simplicity.

ROMANS 12:8 KJV

FROM THE FATHER'S HEART

My child, life is not as complicated as you might think. You can learn simplicity by living with a single purpose in mind and refusing to hold on to that which might bring harm or interference into your life. Some think that their possessions are for their use only; they forget that everything is still a gift from My hand. Simplicity recognizes that all you have is from Me and must be shared freely with others.

FROM A SEEKING HEART

Lord, You had everything; yet You gave it all away so that we could inherit Your wealth. On earth, You had nothing in material goods; yet You met need after need in the hearts and bodies of people. With single purpose and simple love, You changed the world! I, too, want to live simply and give freely, never holding back for myself what belongs to You anyway. Lord, from this point on, I'm choosing a life of simplicity.

SIMPLE TRUTH

It's not how much we own but how much owns us that makes a difference.

INNOCENCE

"Be as shrewd as snakes and as innocent as doves."

MATTHEW 10:16

FROM THE FATHER'S HEART

My child, do not be afraid when I send you out as My representative. Others need to hear of My love, and you must tell them. You will be like sheep among wolves; many will turn away in apathy, but others will stalk you unmercifully, trying to catch you off guard. I want to develop innocence in you so you will adopt My attitude about sin as your own. Allow into your life only those influences that will edify and strengthen your walk with Me. And never try to steal into enemy territory without Me.

FROM A SEEKING HEART

Lord, while others may sample the delicacies of sin, I cannot. I choose to believe Your Word is my guide and truth for my life. You have wiped my guilty slate clean and replaced it with Your own innocence. May I always see sin through Your eyes, Lord. Keep my heart pure and my eyes open so I can see clearly where to go and what to say. And thank You for Your wisdom and protection whenever I speak Your name.

SIMPLE TRUTH

Whom God has declared innocent, no one can call guilty.

WORSHIPFULNESS

I will bless the LORD at all times;
his praise shall continually be in my mouth.

PSALM 34:1 RSV

FROM THE FATHER'S HEART

My child, many think that worship is the mystical experience that takes place between the Creator and His creation—usually within the structure of a church or synagogue. But worshipfulness is a daily attitude of gratitude and a choice you can make to live in My presence moment by moment in spirit and in truth. You can praise Me with your life, your voice, and your attitude because of what I have done for you, but most of all because of who I am.

FROM A SEEKING HEART

Father, every breath I take, every thought I think, every act I do is a worship experience because You are the focal point. "From the rising of the sun [until] the going down of the same"—that includes *all* times, Lord. It does not mean I am living with a Bible on my chest, isolated from anything and anyone. But throughout the day, I'm so aware that our relationship is what matters. You are that "one thing that's needed," and I want worshipfulness of You to characterize every part and every moment of my life.

SIMPLE TRUTH

True worship is a way of life.

UNIQUENESS

*According as he hath chosen us in him before
the foundation of the world,
that we should be holy and without blame before him in love.*

EPHESIANS 1:4 KJV

FROM THE FATHER'S HEART

My child, I drew the blueprints for your life. I knew you long before you were born. Keep reflecting that uniqueness, and recognize that you are special to Me and that I have chosen you for a special purpose in My world. No one else can fill your shoes or your purpose. Because I love you and have a wonderful plan for your life, you can live joyfully with gratitude. You truly bear the mark of heaven's uniqueness.

FROM A SEEKING HEART

Father, You have convinced me of Your great love for me that is higher than the heavens and deeper than the oceans. And I know that You created all Your children with a special purpose in mind—to honor and glorify You in whatever work we do. My uniqueness is not because I am especially gifted or called to some notable position. I am unique because I belong to You, Lord. I accept Your call on my life. Today I will let that uniqueness shine for You!

SIMPLE TRUTH

Change your world—wherever you are, however you can.

PEACEFULNESS

Great peace have those who love thy law;
nothing can make them stumble.

PSALM 119:165 RSV

FROM THE FATHER'S HEART

My child, you really can face each day with unruffled feathers and a relaxed attitude, no matter what your personality may be. As you trust Me in each situation of your life, I will give you an attitude of peacefulness—so that you know you can handle any problem with My help. My Word will give you a strength and calmness of spirit that will allow nothing to interrupt your relationship with Me. It is a peace that passes all human understanding.

FROM A SEEKING HEART

Lord, some days I can almost smell the salty ocean spray and feel the hairs on my head standing tall—the same way Peter did when his peaceful boat rocked dangerously in the churning sea. But that was *before* You calmed the stormy winds and *before* Peter understood who You really were. I know peacefulness will characterize my life only as I trust You implicitly and take every care before You, refusing to worry or fear. Lord, let peace reign daily, no matter what the circumstances I face!

SIMPLE TRUTH

If Jesus is in the boat, we can always stay afloat.

GRATEFULNESS

*Praise the LORD. Give thanks to the LORD,
for he is good; his love endures forever.*

PSALM 106:1

FROM THE FATHER'S HEART

My child, just like a gratified parent, when you show a grateful spirit, I want to bless you even more. Realizing the magnitude of My goodness to you will cause you to respond with gratefulness. In turn, a truly thankful heart will compel you to give Me back not just a part but all that you have and all that you are out of love. The best relationship cannot thrive without love and true appreciation.

FROM A SEEKING HEART

Lord, 365 days and 365 ways could never be enough to say "Thank You" for Your goodness, Your faithfulness, Your love, and Your mercy. And to think, Your love is one that does not end tomorrow but endures forever! How can I ever say thanks enough? Lord, I don't always show it, but I truly want You to know it: I am so thankful for You and all that You have given to me. I choose to let gratefulness begin and end each of my days.

SIMPLE TRUTH

*Real gratitude of the heart is shown by giving our all,
not just a part.*

NEIGHBORLINESS

"Love your neighbor as yourself."

MATTHEW 19:19

FROM THE FATHER'S HEART

My child, someone once asked Me, "Who is my neighbor?" How would you answer that? Wherever I place you, there will be people in need. Those who show true neighborliness will treat others in the same way they want to be treated. It is accepting others as My special creations, going the second mile—not just filling obligations—and above all, always looking for opportunities to show My love.

FROM A SEEKING HEART

Lord, You mirrored a lifestyle that said every person was Your neighbor. You turned away no one with a real need. And You always made time for people. You died for everyone because You loved *all* people. How can I refuse to help a person when You have given me the means to do it? How can I fail to love someone that You have loved first? I go to great pains to care for my own needs—let me do the same for my neighbor. What good can I do for someone today, Lord?

SIMPLE TRUTH

Listen with your heart; speak with your life.

LOVELINESS

He has made everything beautiful in its time.

ECCLESIASTES 3:11

FROM THE FATHER'S HEART

My child, do you often feel like a broken piece of pottery? Remember when you are on the Potter's wheel, I am developing the character of loveliness in you as a result of My breaking and shaping process. The choice is yours to remain in My Master Potter hands. If you do, I will take great care in making you a beautiful reflection of My image.

FROM A SEEKING HEART

Father, there are unpleasant times in my life when I, indeed, feel like there is a whole lot of shaking and breaking going on. Some occurs because of my own sin and its resulting consequences. But as the Master Potter, You take all of my cracks and weaknesses and mold them into something beautiful. Father, I want the loveliness of Your character to reflect in my life. I choose to submit again and again to Your shaping process.

SIMPLE TRUTH

Every person is a masterpiece to God.

INVISIBILITY

He must increase, but I must decrease.

JOHN 3:30 KJV

FROM THE FATHER'S HEART

My child, remember that I have the power to exalt or demote. When you care more about My name than your own, you are learning something about invisibility. That's when you are glorifying Me instead of yourself. Whether I place you in the limelight or behind the scenes does not matter. With invisibility, you can honor Me and give Me the credit for any good that might come from your life.

FROM A SEEKING HEART

Lord, others couldn't help seeing Your visibility when You taught the multitudes, healed the sick, and raised the dead. Yet invisibility describes Your single purpose to glorify Your heavenly Father in everything. Forgive me when I've cared too much about who gets the credit or whether life is fair to me. It's my desire to grow more invisible—so that You might become more visible in my life.

SIMPLE TRUTH

The more of Him I see, the less there is of me.

ASSURANCE

*Let us draw near to God with a sincere heart
in full assurance of faith.*

HEBREWS 10:22

FROM THE FATHER'S HEART

My child, is your heart filled with doubts? Have others tried to persuade you that nothing is certain in this world but death and taxes? I want to give you assurance—so you can believe that what I say is true and live in the boldness of My Word. Be assured that I love you, that I care for you, and that I will always be with you. You can rest in My promises because I have an unbroken track record of faithfulness.

FROM A SEEKING HEART

Father, who can I trust if I can't trust You? I have tried Your promises, and I have read Your words of comfort. There are things I don't understand at times—Your timing, Your silence, and Your ways that are higher than my ways. But You have given me the assurance that I can come boldly to You anytime day or night, and You will hear me. You've assured me that once I invite You into my heart, I am Your child forever. I choose to look not at how I feel or the circumstances around me but at Your Word.

SIMPLE TRUTH

What God says, God does.

POTENTIAL

*He who began a good work in you will carry it on
to completion until the day of Christ Jesus.*

PHILIPPIANS 1:6

FROM THE FATHER'S HEART

My child, I am not through with you yet. Will you recognize your potential the way I do? Despite your faults and weaknesses, I see endless possibilities! You are responsible for developing the raw talent I give you, but I will bless the work you do for Me. Will you rest in My hands and allow Me the privilege of determining the finished product?

FROM A SEEKING HEART

Father, just when I'm ready to throw in the towel, You wash my feet and dry my tears, offering words of encouragement and hope. Somehow You take my mistakes and all my foolish efforts and show me a better way. You see something in me that I cannot see for myself. Lord, help me catch a glimpse again of Your potential for my life. I am so grateful that You never give up on me. I am the one who needs to wash *Your* feet with my tears of gratitude.

SIMPLE TRUTH

God always finishes to perfection what He starts.

MATURITY

That we henceforth be no more children. . .
but speaking the truth in love, may grow up into him
in all things, which is the head, even Christ.

EPHESIANS 4:14–15 KJV

FROM THE FATHER'S HEART

My child, some think the older they get, the more they know—and the less they need to learn. That's childish thinking. You will develop maturity by cultivating a teachable spirit—the ability to receive what is valuable and helpful in life and to reject the things that are harmful. As you feed yourself with My Word, I will help you handle each situation you encounter with patience and wisdom.

FROM A SEEKING HEART

Father, I can identify with the prophet Jeremiah when he said, "I am just a child!" I feel like I will always be in Your training school. Yet I know there is a difference in always learning but never coming to the truth. And there is a difference between acting childish and being teachable. I want to learn maturity, Lord—to think and act wisely yet constantly acknowledge that I have no wisdom of my own, only what You give me. Only a fool would reject the Master Teacher!

SIMPLE TRUTH
Age doesn't give wisdom; God does.

PRAYERFULNESS

*And pray in the Spirit on all occasions with all kinds
of prayers and requests.*

EPHESIANS 6:18

FROM THE FATHER'S HEART

My child, do you really want to make a difference in your
world? No matter what your gifts or talents, no matter
where I've placed you, there is something I want all My
children to do. I want to develop prayerfulness in you so
that you can stay tuned to heaven's heartbeat and keep
aware of the needs in My world. When you are faithful to
pray, I can turn mountains into pebbles and storms into
showers of blessing.

FROM A SEEKING HEART

Lord, prayer was a lifeline for You to Your heavenly Father.
You constantly stole away to recharge and to draw strength.
And when You prayed for Your disciples, You prayed for
me—those who would come after Your ascension. Lord, I
know that my prayers are like perfumed sacrifices You receive joyfully when I pray according to Your will. I will keep
prayerfulness a priority in my life. If I am going to wear out,
I would rather wear out in the knees.

SIMPLE TRUTH
Worries cease when I'm on my knees.

MODESTY

Do not think of yourself more highly than you ought, but rather think of yourself with sober judgment, in accordance with the measure of faith God has given you.

ROMANS 12:3

FROM THE FATHER'S HEART

My child, what I want for you is not a big head but a big heart. As I reminded My children in Scripture, you enjoy things for which you have not worked and earn that which you do not deserve. Yet I choose to bless you because I love you. Develop an attitude of modesty, a dependency upon Me for every detail of your life. Recognize daily that I am your source of life, and give Me credit for all that I am and all that I do. If you boast, let your boast be in Me.

FROM A SEEKING HEART

Lord, not even the clothes I wear or the home I share belongs to me. My possessions, my health, my accomplishments—even my family are gifts on loan from You. How can I boast about something that does not even belong to me? Lord, I am totally dependent on You and am nothing apart from You. May modesty always adorn my spirit, Lord, so that anything I do calls attention only to You.

SIMPLE TRUTH

It's often hard to see when the spotlight is on me.

ALLEGIANCE

"Give to Caesar what is Caesar's, and to God what is God's."

MATTHEW 22:21

FROM THE FATHER'S HEART

My child, be wise about the voices you listen to. I want your sole allegiance—an attitude of thanksgiving for what has been given to you and a determination to make My causes yours. You can choose loyalty to Me, to your country, and to others because of the price that has been paid for your freedom. Make sure you stand for what is right.

FROM A SEEKING HEART

Lord, I do pledge allegiance to You—and to You alone. Because of the price You paid, I have true freedom—a daily hope in the life I now live, a sinful life reconciled to a holy God and a home in heaven when I die. Thank You for that freedom, Lord, and for all the ones who died to make this earthly home a safer place to live. Your concerns are my concerns, Lord, and wherever You lead, I will follow with my allegiance.

SIMPLE TRUTH

A true nation under God is one that is under God's rule.

TENDERNESS

*Be ye kind one to another, tenderhearted,
forgiving one another.*

EPHESIANS 4:32 KJV

FROM THE FATHER'S HEART

My child, before you speak harshly to someone, remember
that every person is of value to Me. I've been a compassionate Father and like a tender mother to you, nursing your
hurts, forgiving your faults, and encouraging you in your
weaknesses. I want you to act with tenderness as well, seeing others as I see them and placing yourself objectively in
their situation. Because I have dealt gently with you, you
can be sensitive to the needs and feelings of others.

FROM A SEEKING HEART

Lord, there are no excuses for the times I've rebuked others
in anger or failed to listen to another's reasons. Who am I
to play God in someone's life? While I can reprove and help
restore one who has sinned, I must do so gently and carefully, always seeking Your wisdom and making sure I am
right with You. Because I want Your character, Lord, and
because I want to reflect You, I choose to respond with tenderness to others—beginning now.

SIMPLE TRUTH

Forgiving is a way of living.

AMIABILITY

*How good and pleasant it is when brothers
live together in unity!*

PSALM 133:1

FROM THE FATHER'S HEART

My child, you do not live alone in this world. You will find
people who will encourage you and those who will make life
difficult for you. But I want to develop in you the gift of
peacemaking—the ability to get along well with all kinds of
people. You can make others feel important and recognize
their worth in Me. And most of all, you can be My ambassador, showing others how to find peace with Me.

FROM A SEEKING HEART

Father, thank You for reminding me often that You died for
the whole world—everyone in it—not just a select few. People *are* important to You. Keep my heart tender and open to
others so I can maintain my integrity but still value the
worth and opinions of others. Whether I agree with someone or not does not give me the right to shun or open fire.
Because of You, I choose amiability and will try to live
peaceably with all.

SIMPLE TRUTH

Love is never "one-sighted."

SINCERITY

Love must be sincere.
Hate what is evil; cling to what is good.

ROMANS 12:9

FROM THE FATHER'S HEART

My child, masks never become My children. What I want in you is a sincere heart. I will develop sincerity in you when you open up each area of your life to Me. Then I can remove those masks of hypocrisy, indifference, and apathy; and you can live transparently and honestly before Me and others. Don't just pretend to love others. Let Me really love them through you.

FROM A SEEKING HEART

Lord, I do cling to You because I know nothing good can come from my heart without You. You know me through and through, and You remind me of how deceptive my own heart really can be. Lord, my desire is to live before You and others with a pure heart, one that does not try to hide or harbor sin, one that says sincerely, "Come on in." Today I choose sincerity and will guard my heart with diligence.

SIMPLE TRUTH

Pretending is for actors, not players.

DEPENDABILITY

*"Whoever can be trusted with very little
can also be trusted with much."*

LUKE 16:10

FROM THE FATHER'S HEART

My child, work is both a gift and a privilege. I want you to
learn dependability so you can take seriously the tasks and
opportunities that I give you to fulfill. With My help, you can
consistently meet the pressures and stresses around you and
be a person upon whom I and others can depend. When I
know I can trust your heart, I delight in giving you even more
responsibility—which means more opportunity to make a
difference for Me.

FROM A SEEKING HEART

Father, when I ask You to expand my territory of influence,
I realize that means I must be faithful in the tasks I already
have as well. I cannot do any of it without You, Lord. Every
time I see roadblocks instead of paths and problems instead
of opportunities, I know I am operating in my own strength.
I choose dependability, Lord. Take what little I have and
help me multiply it for Your glory!

SIMPLE TRUTH

It only takes one person to make a difference.

DELICACY

By the meekness and gentleness of Christ, I appeal to you.

2 CORINTHIANS 10:1

FROM THE FATHER'S HEART

My child, no matter how wrong you think another may be, you must act right in your approach or response to them. You will win more friends and followers of Me through loving admonition than angry opposition. Use delicacy and respond gently rather than reacting harshly. There is a time for everything, but delicacy can remain open to others' feelings and thoughts without stomping on their character. Always ask yourself the question, *What would Jesus say or do?*

FROM A SEEKING HEART

Lord, words in Your mouth were like "apples of gold in pictures of silver." You always spoke boldly with authority; yet delicacy dotted every sentence. Yes, You showed anger when Your Father's reputation was threatened. But You were never out of control. How I need that delicacy in my own life, Lord. Teach me the difference between responding and reacting. It does no good for me to curse the darkness if I fail to reveal the Light in the process.

SIMPLE TRUTH

Dynamite can be used positively or negatively, depending on who holds the controls.

FORCEFULNESS

Faithful are the wounds of a friend.

PROVERBS 27:6 KJV

FROM THE FATHER'S HEART

My child, when your faith or the faith of others is under fire, it is not the time for timidity. When you are tempted to condone wrong or to cower due to fear of rejection, I will enable you to speak honestly. You can be forceful and face the truth without wavering in order to help and restore others. Remember, a true friend will tell you the truth, while an enemy may flatter you in order to win your approval. Deception never pays.

FROM A SEEKING HEART

Father, how easy it is to fall into the trap of winning others' approval. Forgive me for the times I've ignored the opportunity to speak up for You, valuing my own comfort instead of the growing conviction within me. And, when appropriate, help me use forcefulness to speak the truth lovingly to another when it could mean restoration instead of destruction. If I care enough, I will be sensitive to Your Spirit and speak the words You give me.

SIMPLE TRUTH

The truth may not always be popular, but it is always right.

SOUNDNESS

*What you heard from me, keep as the pattern of sound teaching,
with faith and love in Christ Jesus.*

2 TIMOTHY 1:13

FROM THE FATHER'S HEART

My child, never be ashamed of the name "Christian." Guard
carefully in your heart what My Spirit has taught you. I will
develop soundness in you when you remain well grounded in
My teachings. Take care to recognize Me as your supreme
authority, and refuse to accept that which is contrary to the
truth of My Word. Many will claim to know the "truth." But
remember, I am the Truth. And the truth of My words will
set you free.

FROM A SEEKING HEART

Father, what I read from Your Word, I want to do. And in
what I do, I want to honor You. I am convinced that You are
the Truth, and I know that all the principles in Your Word
apply to my life. I will meet with You daily and look for my
life's instructions in the Scriptures. And moment by moment
I will listen for Your Spirit's promptings and teachings so my
faith and love can grow. Your teaching is my pattern for life.
And being grounded in soundness is my choice.

SIMPLE TRUTH
Time with God is time well spent.

YOUTHFULNESS

*Praise the LORD. . .who satisfies your desires with good things
so that your youth is renewed like the eagle's.*

PSALM 103:2, 5

FROM THE FATHER'S HEART

My child, do you want to soar like an eagle instead of hobble
with broken wings? Age has nothing to do with your vitality
in the inner man or woman. Youthfulness is an attitude you
can choose by cultivating gratitude and thanksgiving to Me.
Trust Me to renew your spirit so that your heart can stay
open, tender, and vulnerable to My leadership. Your body
may grow older, but your spirit can grow younger.

FROM A SEEKING HEART

Father, no one wants to grow old before his or her time. But
I know that even the best beauty products and vitamins in the
world cannot make us more spiritual or more youthful inside.
I do choose an attitude of youthfulness by taking responsibility for my attitude. A sour, bitter disposition will age me. The
good things I find in You and the gratitude that wells up
within me may not erase the wrinkles, but it will enlarge the
heart—and give me spirit wings—even in old age.

SIMPLE TRUTH

It is impossible to soar without wings.

WHOLEHEARTEDNESS

I will give thanks to the LORD with my whole heart,
in the company of the upright, in the congregation.

PSALM 111:1 RSV

FROM THE FATHER'S HEART

My child, how do you respond to good news? How do you return another's love? Some of My children have no problem with putting their whole hearts and bodies into cheering for a winning sports team. Why not respond to Me with wholeheartedness by giving Me your total abandonment? You do that when you choose Me above all other loves and direct all your energies toward whatever is important to Me.

FROM A SEEKING HEART

Father, may every fiber in my being cry out with thanksgiving to You. You are *everything* to me! Every other interest in life seems so unimportant when compared to You. Lord, forgive my halfhearted efforts in the past. I am so in love with You, Lord, and recognize that without You, there really is only half a heart in me. I want my praise, my thanksgiving, my work, my life, and my every expression to be totally abandoned wholeheartedly to You—so that I can make You known everywhere I go.

SIMPLE TRUTH
No one wants to hear, "I love you with half of my heart."

THRIFTINESS

*Better a little with the fear of the LORD
than great wealth with turmoil.*

PROVERBS 15:16

FROM THE FATHER'S HEART

My child, things can weigh you down like an anchor in the water. I would love to give you thriftiness so you would have the ability to concentrate on quality without quantity. By doing so, you value things less in order to free yourself from the entanglement and power of materialism. Your ultimate objective? So you can love others and serve Me more effectively.

FROM A SEEKING HEART

Father, You have taught me that things don't really matter and never last anyway. Yet materialism lures us with every neon flash, every clever advertisement, and every deceptive scheme. In reality, it seems that the more things we own, the more problems we create. Things break. Things cost. Things steal time and affection. Lord, I am committing myself to thriftiness. I will want less and give more. And I will use Your wisdom before spending Your wealth on anything foolish. Most of all, I choose to make significant eternal investments with more time and money for Your work.

SIMPLE TRUTH

There is a difference between being cheap and being thrifty.

INTIMACY

Draw near to God and he will draw near to you.

JAMES 4:8 RSV

FROM THE FATHER'S HEART

My child, more than anything else, I want us to have an intimate relationship with each other. Can you imagine a child never knowing his father? You cannot expect to maintain fellowship with Me and harbor sin in your heart. Draw near to Me daily, and let Me build intimacy in you—a close, intentional relationship with Me. I will draw you to Myself as you place Me first in your life and deliberately spend time getting to know Me.

FROM A SEEKING HEART

Father, through Christ's death and resurrection, You provided a door for intimacy with You. Knowing You and loving You is my heart's chief desire. Two marriage partners cannot live joyfully without daily communion and intimacy. Likewise, I must intentionally choose to draw near to You. By faith, I choose to resist my enemy, who would try to steal away my affection from You; and I will run to You daily to bask in Your love. Lord, I cannot function without You!

SIMPLE TRUTH

A heart desperate for love will go to any lengths to find it.

PREPAREDNESS

Always be prepared to give an answer to everyone who asks
you to give the reason for the hope that you have.
But do this with gentleness and respect.

1 PETER 3:15

FROM THE FATHER'S HEART

My child, I have great plans for you every day—more wonderful than you can possibly imagine! Are you prepared to
receive them? You can develop preparedness by letting Me
cleanse your life daily, confessing every known sin, and
making yourself available for My disposal. With My Word
in your heart and My love in your life, you will be ready for
any divine appointment.

FROM A SEEKING HEART

Father, my commitment to You is to show up every morning, faithfully awaiting Your instructions, basking in Your
presence, and learning to love You a little more. In the past
I have attempted to walk through the day without first
waiting on You—and, like a soldier unprepared for battle, I
suffered the consequences. Lord, preparedness is something
I want—and choose—for my life every day!

SIMPLE TRUTH

Discipline is the price of excellence.

ENCOURAGEMENT

*Let us consider how we may spur one another on toward love
and good deeds. Let us. . .encourage one another.*

HEBREWS 10:24–25

FROM THE FATHER'S HEART

My child, words can be weapons or gifts. Everyone needs to
know he or she is of worth and value to Me. You can help others discover that truth. Learn to use encouragement—focusing your eyes and heart on the needs of others. Choose words
or actions that will bring joy and hope. As I fill you with those
same qualities, you can share them with others who desperately need encouragement—"courage within."

FROM A SEEKING HEART

Lord, like a Barnabas to Paul—and like You have been for
me—I want to come alongside others and be the wind beneath their wings. I want to lift up the fallen, encourage the
fainthearted, and pray for the discouraged. Today I will
choose words—and actions—that say to another, "You are
important to me and to God. How can I help you today? I
really care about you." Lord, I will be sensitive to Your Spirit
and listen for the words so greatly needed by a discouraged
heart. I choose to be Your encourager.

SIMPLE TRUTH
One word can make or break a spirit.

DIGNITY

We are therefore Christ's ambassadors.

2 CORINTHIANS 5:20

FROM THE FATHER'S HEART

My child, not only do your words and actions affect others positively or negatively, but they also reflect on Me. While I understand your weaknesses, I do not excuse thoughtlessness and deliberate sin. I want to develop in you a sense of dignity so you can feel the pride and honor of being My personal representative. You can be responsible for your actions, thoughts, and words, which will ultimately reflect upon the One you represent.

FROM A SEEKING HEART

Lord, how You carried Yourself with dignity on earth! Always a model ambassador of Your heavenly Father, You showed us the perfect example. Being known as a "Christ One"—Christian—and ambassador for You may cause us to feel like we are living in a fishbowl. Curious eyes gawk and speculate on what kind of "fish" we are. But knowing we are Your personal representatives also creates an accountability we need. Lord, I will wear the name "Christian" today with dignity. It is an honor to represent the One I love.

SIMPLE TRUTH

People in glass houses can reflect the Son clearly.

SUBMISSION

Submit to one another out of reverence for Christ.

EPHESIANS 5:21

FROM THE FATHER'S HEART

My child, if everyone tried to be in charge, the world would be in chaos. I created My world with order and with a chain of authority in place. Not only that, your respect of My authority brings order to your own life. I will develop a spirit of submission in you as you show willingness to trust the ideas, judgments, or actions of others that affect you personally. When you submit to Me first, I will help you to yield to others who have been placed in authority over you.

FROM A SEEKING HEART

Lord, once again, if I really want to know "What would Jesus do?" and then duplicate Your actions, I must learn submissiveness. I only know You, Lord—and that Your submissiveness to Your heavenly Father resulted in my life and freedom. While I may not agree with everyone in authority over me, I can agree with You to willingly submit myself to You first and then to come under the proper authority You have placed over me—for my own success and protection—but also that Your name might ultimately be honored as well.

SIMPLE TRUTH
   A body with two heads never really knows who is in charge.

HELPFULNESS

*" 'Whatever you did for one of the least of these brothers of mine,
you did for me.' "*

MATTHEW 25:40

FROM THE FATHER'S HEART

My child, I love to reach into another's heart through you.
You have My character—and My Spirit—living in you. You
can really make a difference in people's lives. How? Have
you loved the unlovely? Visited the sick? Clothed the poor?
Fed the hungry? Encouraged the weak? When you give
your time to Me to use as I wish, you are developing helpfulness. And when you choose unselfishly to help others, it
is the same as showing love and kindness to Me.

FROM A SEEKING HEART

Lord, can You really use me to help others? Here are my
hands, my heart, my mind, and my feet. Extend my influence any way You see fit. Whether it is nurturing my own
precious children, ushering a neighbor into my own food
pantry, or "visiting" and helping to free others whose minds
and hearts are imprisoned behind bars of sin, fear, or discouragement—Lord, use me. I choose helpfulness that will
touch not only the hearts of others but Your heart as well.

SIMPLE TRUTH

Take time to find a way to be kind.

VALOR

Through God we shall do valiantly:
for he it is that shall tread down our enemies.

PSALM 60:12 KJV

FROM THE FATHER'S HEART

My child, do you tire of hiding from your enemies in the "winepress" of your heart? I visualize the possibilities you cannot see. You can become a person of valor by taking the offensive in My strength. Whenever you are facing battles with enemies of fear, doubt, or discouragement, I will give you supernatural courage to withstand all of their obstacles. I will take care of your enemies and give you a new hiding place—in Me.

FROM A SEEKING HEART

Father, trying to defend myself against my enemies wears me out. I must learn the tactics of good offense as well. Yet my most valiant defense and offense will fail unless You are my quarterback. The next time I face a notorious lineup, I will use valor, trusting in Your strength, not my own. Not only that, I will make sure I play on a team that offers accountability and backup and who takes their instructions from You alone.

SIMPLE TRUTH

I may not play in the Super Bowl, but I can be super-
bold for Christ.

RIGHTEOUSNESS

God made him who had no sin to be sin for us,
so that in him we might become the righteousness of God.

2 CORINTHIANS 5:21

FROM THE FATHER'S HEART

Do you have trouble deciding what clothes to wear each day? Remember that righteousness is My personal garment of forgiveness—a gift I have given to you so you could be perfectly acceptable to Me. It is My guarantee of entry into My throne room. Accept this gift joyfully, and wear it proudly. I paid for it with My life.

FROM A SEEKING HEART

Lord, this is a mystery I've never understood. I know there is no righteousness—no good thing—in me or in what I do myself. And yet there is no way I could know God without righteousness. That You would give me this gift through Your death on the cross is magnificent and beyond my comprehension. I choose to wear this garment of righteousness daily, knowing it is the mark of a Christian.

SIMPLE TRUTH

"Rightness" with God gives us new strength to make
other relationships "right."

DEXTERITY

*"Bless all his skills, O LORD,
and be pleased with the work of his hands."*

DEUTERONOMY 33:11

FROM THE FATHER'S HEART

My child, I didn't ask you to be the best or most skilled in
your trade or occupation. I just want you to serve Me joyfully
and skillfully, using well the talents I have given you. Dexterity will come when you offer your hands and heart to Me. I
will then turn them into instruments of praise and adoration.
You will be amazed at what we can build together.

FROM A SEEKING HEART

Father, at times I feel as if I am "all thumbs" and accomplishing nothing for You. That's when I realize I've been
trying on my own again. You made these hands; You gave
me the skills to use them wisely. God, grant me dexterity
with hands like Yours that bless, not curse; that build up,
not tear down; that help, not hinder; that serve, not withdraw; that lift in praise, not surrender in self-pity. Lord, use
these hands to make a difference for You!

SIMPLE TRUTH

Hands that bless others are hands that bless the Lord.

FREEDOM

"Then you will know the truth, and the truth will set you free."

JOHN 8:32

FROM THE FATHER'S HEART

My child, would you want to return to a life of bondage? It is for freedom that I died for you and set you free! Freedom offers you opportunity for truth, wisdom, and responsibility. This is a life lived totally under the control of My Spirit, a pearl of great price. You can show your gratitude to Me with a life dedicated to Me and the betterment of My world. My grace gives you freedom!

FROM A SEEKING HEART

Lord, thank You for the freedom You have given me—room to grow, grace to live, courage to change. But occasionally I still find myself believing age-old lies and succumbing to habitual patterns that hold me in bondage and cut off the Spirit's working in my life. True freedom will come when I receive the truth You reveal to me, Lord—truth about myself, truth about You and Your Word. Open my eyes, Lord, and help me discern deception from the real truth—so I might experience *real* freedom.

SIMPLE TRUTH

*In order to experience freedom, we must give God
freedom to change our hearts.*

REST

Rest in the LORD, and wait patiently for him.

PSALM 37:7 KJV

FROM THE FATHER'S HEART

My child, are you tired of running? Do you find yourself breathless and unable to cope with daily challenges? I will give you rest if you will wait on Me daily. Start and end your day with My words, and throughout the day let My thoughts fuel your thoughts. You can turn to Me in troubling times and know that I will fill your spirit with a calm peace and assurance that I am in control.

FROM A SEEKING HEART

Lord, chaos comes like an unexpected roadblock, and I often feel as if every road is a dead-end street. I know You allow disturbing circumstances into my life to teach me how to wait patiently, but I have trouble "getting it" sometimes. You continually rested in Your Father, and when ugly mobs threatened You and death grew near, You still patiently waited for God to complete His work in You. I need that rest, Lord. I choose today to listen, to wait, to rest—and to nest—in the shelter of Your arms.

SIMPLE TRUTH

All of us need resting—and more nesting—in the Father's love.

PERSUASION

I know whom I have believed,
and am persuaded that he is able to keep that
which I have committed unto him against that day.

2 TIMOTHY 1:12 KJV

FROM THE FATHER'S HEART

My child, who do you believe that I am? With persuasion comes the strong belief that I am who I say I am. You no longer need to question, but you can believe the testimony of My Word with the validity of your experience. When you are fully convinced of who I am, you will share My message freely and joyfully with others.

FROM A SEEKING HEART

Lord, my heart agrees with the confession of my mouth. You are indeed the Christ. You are the King of Kings. You are the Messiah. You are everything You ever said You would be. Lord, let persuasion always be rooted deeply in my heart, so when others ask me, I can readily share my deepest love—and talk to others about the awesome, magnificent God I know!

SIMPLE TRUTH

God never forgets what we commit to Him.

LOYALTY

*Many a man proclaims his own loyalty,
but a faithful man who can find?*

PROVERBS 20:6 RSV

FROM THE FATHER'S HEART

My child, what if you had been Job? Abraham? Mary? Would you have treated Me as they did? How do you hold up under stress? Loyalty will develop as you learn to see beyond the surface experiences of life and understand the crusty challenges of life and the hard knocks of reality. Loyalty chooses to remain faithful to the cause of Christ no matter what the consequences.

FROM A SEEKING HEART

Lord, I can do no less than observe Your own life on earth to find my example of loyalty. To please the Father, to carry out His wishes, to obey at all costs—these drove You to complete Your Father's will. Because You loved me, You saw the end result—my salvation—and Your loyalty never wavered. I, too, want to choose faithfulness at all costs, Lord. Help me keep heaven on my mind and the eternal destiny of others so loyalty will characterize me as well.

SIMPLE TRUTH

*Beyond the veil, only God can tell what wonders wait
for us.*

WISDOM

The fear of the LORD is the beginning of wisdom.

PROVERBS 9:10 KJV

FROM THE FATHER'S HEART

My child, I never intended for you to make decisions on your own. Freedom of choice, yes. You are not a robot. But you will never succeed unless you enlist My help. I created you and know what is best for you. When you choose to reverence and respect Me, giving Me first place in your life, I will protect you with wisdom. With wisdom, you can see life through My eyes and make decisions based upon My omniscient insights.

FROM A SEEKING HEART

Father, You are wisdom personified. Forgive me for the times I've fallen simply because I looked away. Pride lured me into thinking I could handle situations over my head. Instead of consulting You and listening to You, I plunged headlong into disaster. You have restored the fear of God in my life. I choose to think before I act, to pray before I decide, and to take You with me everywhere I go. I long for wisdom, Lord, that I might reflect Your true character.

SIMPLE TRUTH

Better to be wise than sorry.

FEARLESSNESS

There is no fear in love. But perfect love drives out fear.

1 John 4:18

From the Father's Heart

My child, how long will you continue to hide in the shadows? I can deal with every chickenhearted fear that enters your heart. I have not given you that spirit of fear but one of love and wholeness. Isn't it time to trust My power and run to the Light? Fearlessness comes when you access My perfect love. In Me, you can find strength and power to overcome hatred, fear, and doubt as you allow Me to work out My will in your life.

From a Seeking Heart

Father, I admit I do not understand Your "perfect" love, but I accept it as a true, undeserved gift. Those times when I've allowed Your love to push back the curtains and expose every inch of my selfish heart, Your love has poured in like a dam that has been opened. Fear is swallowed up in a torrent of gratitude—and in those holy moments, I feel fearless as a lion, yet docile as a lamb. Lord, keep pushing away the shadows. I will not return to fear. I choose to let fearlessness find a permanent home in my heart as Your perfect love lights up my life.

Simple Truth

When we live under the shadow of the Almighty, all other shadows flee.

PURPOSEFULNESS

*Then make my joy complete by being like-minded,
having the same love, being one in spirit and purpose.*

PHILIPPIANS 2:2

FROM THE FATHER'S HEART

My child, why stuff your life with pages of endless, meaningless activities, with no margin and no real meaning? I have a special plan for each of My children, designed for you since birth. When you let My goals direct everything you do, you will discover purposefulness. Give your life to Me each day as a clean page, purposing to honor Me, and I will make your life an open book that will glorify Me.

FROM A SEEKING HEART

Lord, since the day I first met You, I knew You would turn my life upside down. You have given me a purpose in living and a reason for thanksgiving. As You weed out the cluttered motives of my heart, I find new direction—and the peace of knowing You are in control. You have given me purposefulness. Lord, will You write on my life volumes of good things that will touch Your heart and others' hearts, too?

SIMPLE TRUTH

God created us on purpose—with purpose—for His purpose.

PATIENCE

Encourage the timid, help the weak, be patient with everyone.

1 THESSALONIANS 5:14

FROM THE FATHER'S HEART

My child, do you still wonder why I send different people into your life? Do you not understand the purpose of "bad days" and endless challenges? If you want to bear My character, you must learn what patience is all about. It is waiting on My timetable, resting in Me, and accepting the human frailties of others. Because I am patient with you, you can give others time and tenderness as well.

FROM A SEEKING HEART

Lord, if ever there was a quality You mirrored for us, it is patience. If I had been thrown into the situations You were, I know I would have lost it every time. But Your love and compassion for people override any impatience, Lord. Help me see people like You see them; love them like You love them; and to remember that others have weaknesses just like my own. I accept those different situations—and irregular people—as lessons to teach me more about You. And I choose to exercise patience as Your Spirit calms mine daily.

SIMPLE TRUTH

It only takes a minute—to put some kindness in it.

ASPIRATION

*Delight yourself in the LORD and he will give you
the desires of your heart.*

PSALM 37:4

FROM THE FATHER'S HEART

My child, as you abandon your own interests and seek My
ways, I will not disappoint you. When you express an intense longing and desire to know Me and to be used in My
service, I know you have aspiration. As you place your desires in My hand, I will show you My plan for your life. And
when you truly delight yourself in Me, My desires will become your desires.

FROM A SEEKING HEART

Lord, it is You I want—not a fabricated set of man-made
rules, not a list of do-it-yourself tools—but You, only You.
My joy and my delight is to do Your will no matter what. I
can design a dream, Lord, but only as I resign it to You will
it ever stand a chance of reality. Reassign to me the desires of
Your heart, Lord—so that Your dreams can become my
dreams. My heart's aspiration is to know and love You deeply.

SIMPLE TRUTH

*Always anticipate something to do for Christ today
and something to do for Christ tomorrow.*

STRENGTH

I can do everything through him who gives me strength.

PHILIPPIANS 4:13

FROM THE FATHER'S HEART

My child, I hear your cries of "I can't." Of course you can't—
not in your own natural strength. Can you move a mountain
alone? You will fail with every attempt. I have given you
every supernatural thing you need for success. Real strength
comes in living life through My power by not depending
solely on your own abilities or wisdom. As you trust Me
with your life, nothing will be impossible because I will be
working through you.

FROM A SEEKING HEART

Lord, in Your strength I can run through barriers and leap
over walls. In Your strength I can scale great heights and
cross over wide rivers. In Your strength I can encourage the
weak and lift up the fallen. In Your strength I can speak
Your name boldly and bear witness to the faithfulness of a
great and powerful God. In Your strength—and with Your
strength—everything is possible if it fits Your plan, Lord.
Today I can—and will—choose to walk in the strength You
have given me.

SIMPLE TRUTH

"Can" your can'ts, and open your "cans."

MOTIVATION

For to me, to live is Christ.

PHILIPPIANS 1:21

FROM THE FATHER'S HEART

My child, when you were young, what motivated your actions? As a little child, didn't you long to please your earthly father and win his approval? As you grew older, you often let others' approval influence your thoughts and actions. But when you said yes to Me, you surrendered those motives for a greater one. Whatever drives you in life will ultimately determine your usefulness. Always let Me and My love for you become your supreme motivation.

FROM A SEEKING HEART

Father, because I know You, I can greet the dawn of a new day with a smile on my lips and a song in my heart. Because You know me, I can rejoice in the work You have assigned me and rest in the promise of its value. Because I love You, I can't do enough to show my gratitude. Because You love me, I am compelled to share the good news of Your grace and mercy. You *are* my motivation, Lord.

SIMPLE TRUTH

Without Him, I can do nothing. With Him, I can do anything He asks me to.

QUIETNESS

He makes me lie down in green pastures,
he leads me beside quiet waters.

PSALM 23:2

FROM THE FATHER'S HEART

My child, I do not want to force you to lie down in green pastures. I would rather lead you there. When life tries to pull
you under, remember My rest. Like a peaceful mountain
stream, your life will flow quietly and calmly as you place your
trust in Me. When you trust Me, I will encourage and
strengthen your heart. I will bring quietness to your soul.

FROM A SEEKING HEART

Father, how I need Your quiet Spirit! Even when I desperately seek that rest, life has a way of sneaking up and stealing
the hammock right out from under me! But in Your great
wisdom, You have provided all Your children with green pastures. You promise not just to plant the green, grassy knolls
but to *lead* me to that place so my soul, body, and spirit can
find quietness. Today I choose to wait on You, Lord. Lead
me to those green pastures—and the spirit of quietness for
my life.

SIMPLE TRUTH

Quiet places bring happy faces when God is there, too.

ACCESSIBILITY

Show me the way I should go, for to you I lift up my soul.

PSALM 143:8

FROM THE FATHER'S HEART

My child, are you indeed willing to follow Me—wherever? You don't have to fear the "whatever" or "whenever." You can trust My plans for you. They are only for good and not to harm you. I will give you accessibility when you make your life available and open to Me, to go wherever I want to lead you. Following Me will require making some difficult choices, but you can look to Me for direction and purpose.

FROM A SEEKING HEART

Lord, You never hid from Your Father. You made Yourself totally accessible to His plans for You. How could a Savior like that lead me anywhere but to good places? Lord, I do choose accessibility. My heart's desire is to follow You, even if it means discomfort or suffering along the way. As long as I know You have ordained the paths and the destination— and not me in my own stubborn nature—I can even learn Your lessons from any temporary pain. I know Your ultimate goal is to bless me and make my character like Yours.

SIMPLE TRUTH

We don't need to know the path; we just need to know the Way.

RESIGNATION

"Father, if you are willing, take this cup from me;
yet not my will, but yours be done."

LUKE 22:42

FROM THE FATHER'S HEART

My child, can you walk a step farther into the complete trust of your Father? There will be times when it will seem as if My back is turned. But that's not true. Because of My holiness, I turn My back on sin but not on My children. You will know the spirit of resignation when you can honestly say, "Thy will be done, Lord." This is a choice to believe that My ways, though different from yours, are always best—regardless of the outcome.

FROM A SEEKING HEART

Lord, how could You resign Your kingly position in heaven—and choose to die for the whole world? You gave up everything for me so that I could have everything in You. I, too, want to be willing to cry, "Thy will be done!" It won't always be easy—this spirit of resignation—but Your promises are without fail. What we surrender, You return a hundredfold to us. I trust You to determine how the purpose of my life will shake out. In pain or in gain, I resign myself to Your perfect will, Lord.

SIMPLE TRUTH
Wherever He leads is a safe place to be.

SYMPATHY

Praise be to. . .the God of all comfort, who comforts us in
all our troubles, so that we can comfort those in any trouble
with the comfort we ourselves have received from God.

2 CORINTHIANS 1:3–4

FROM THE FATHER'S HEART

My child, when I allow you to go through sorrow or difficulties,
I am opening other areas for joy in your life. Never waste your
suffering. I want to form the gift of sympathy in your heart. Receiving My comfort and love, like treasures in dark places,
will enable you to reinvest those treasures—by helping others
with the same comfort and tenderness I have given to you.

FROM A SEEKING HEART

Lord, I admit I do not like suffering. But I still hear Your
whispers in the dark, echoing through my pain: "I still love
you." Somewhere, a lonely person waits in despair; long wea-
ried from struggling, heart broken over loss or pain. You have
prepared me for that someone so that I can say to that person
with confidence, "I know what you're going through. God has
not forgotten you!" And even when I don't know—You do,
Lord. Father, fill my heart with sympathy for those who need
Your healing restoration.

SIMPLE TRUTH

Feeling others' sorrow will help them face tomorrow.

TENACITY

Prove all things; hold fast that which is good.

1 THESSALONIANS 5:21 KJV

FROM THE FATHER'S HEART

My child, your faith speaks loudest when you are under fire.
I will develop tenacity in you when you refuse to let go of Me
and your determination to hold on to everything helpful and
edifying in your life. In the testing of your faith and in the
trials of your life, you can trust Me no matter what happens,
even if all others forsake you. I will never leave you.

FROM A SEEKING HEART

Lord, why would I turn loose of the one thing that keeps
me going? Like Jacob wrestling with the angel, I will not let
go of You, Lord. You are too precious, and my love is too
strong to give up now. Even in the tough times—especially
in the tough times—I choose tenacity, Lord. Faith in You
never disappoints!

SIMPLE TRUTH

Keep a firm grip on God.

ENTHUSIASM

This is the day the LORD has made;
let us rejoice and be glad in it.

PSALM 118:24

FROM THE FATHER'S HEART

My child, you will not find your daily energy in a box of cereal, nor will you uncover joy in possessions or trophies. Enthusiasm is something that wells up from the inside out— a desire to live life to the fullest. You can celebrate each day that I have given you with excitement, joy, and love and make the most of every opportunity for Me. Today may be the only day you have. Live it enthusiastically, and live it well.

FROM A SEEKING HEART

Father, the world's best vitamins can't energize me like the joy of Your Spirit. Knowing You is a natural high that makes me want to shout in the morning and dance throughout the day. What an exciting way to live—not knowing what to expect but finding my expectation and joy in You! I know You have given every day as a gift for me to live for You; therefore, I choose to live it with enthusiasm.

SIMPLE TRUTH

Dance to the rhythm of heaven's music—even if we dance alone.

BRILLIANCE

*"You are the light of the world.
A city on a hill cannot be hidden."*

MATTHEW 5:14

FROM THE FATHER'S HEART

My child, you are My mirror—a reflection of Me wherever you go. When your life is clean and pure before Me, you can let your light shine through you so that others can see not you but the One who lives in you—Jesus. Keep the Son shining through your mirror, My child, and you will experience the brilliance that I want for all My children.

FROM A SEEKING HEART

Lord, I have nothing of my own to show. If You have placed me on a hill—or on a top shelf—any brilliance that comes through will be because of You. Your light shines brighter, Lord, when mine is on dim. Yet I know You have given me gifts and talents and a work to do for You. As I choose to give You credit and glory in all I do, my "light" will point others to the true Light. Lord, I do want brilliance to characterize my life.

SIMPLE TRUTH

The most brilliant diamonds are the ones with the most cuts and clarity.

VIBRANCY

*The righteous flourish like the palm tree, and grow like a cedar
in Lebanon. They are planted in the house of the LORD,
they flourish in the courts of our God.*

PSALM 92:12–13 RSV

FROM THE FATHER'S HEART

My child, how long you live is not up to you and really
doesn't matter in My scheme of things. I will give you
vibrancy—a quality of life that allows you to live fully and
completely when you place your life in My hands. Whether
you live to be twenty-five or ninety-five, you can plant your
roots into the soil of My love. I will then use you as I see fit.

FROM A SEEKING HEART

Father, whether I *feel* like I'm flourishing or not, I know You
are at work in me, establishing my root system and nour-
ishing me daily. I will do my part to water, cultivate, and
feed on Your Word daily so that vibrancy can truly characterize my life. I am not asking for longevity unless that's
Your desire. But I do want to live close to the source of my
strength and successfully complete Your purpose for my life.

SIMPLE TRUTH

Before a flower can grow, the seed must first die.

RESTRAINT

*We who are strong ought to bear with the failings
of the weak and not to please ourselves.*

ROMANS 15:1

FROM THE FATHER'S HEART

My child, I have given you great freedom, but do not use
that liberty for selfish reasons. Exercise restraint by carefully
watching what you do or say so that you do not cause someone else to stumble or bring shame to My name. Restraint
makes allowances for the beliefs of others while being careful not to violate your own convictions.

FROM A SEEKING HEART

Lord, I have been in the position of watching others—and
gleaning from them. I have been the weaker one trying to
learn from a stronger one. But as I grow in You, I accept the
responsibility that now others read me like their Bible. How I
want to interpret Your truths accurately through my life!
Lord, I will use restraint not only in my actions but also in my
judgment of others. My desire is to please You, not myself.

SIMPLE TRUTH

What others see in our mirrors always reflects on us.

PHILANTHROPY

*You will be made rich in every way so that you can
be generous on every occasion.*

2 CORINTHIANS 9:11

FROM THE FATHER'S HEART

My child, I need to circulate My wealth—and I have chosen My children to do so for Me. Will you be a vessel I can use? I want to give you philanthropy—and let Me distribute My wealth through you for My glory. When I show you genuine needs in others, you can then respond with generous heart and hands because of what I have done for you. That gives Me great pleasure.

FROM A SEEKING HEART

Father, what a miraculous plan You have devised for meeting the needs of others! Forgive me at times for questioning Your provisions and for neglecting decisions to help others in need. You do not give me extra blessings to hoard. You have more than met my needs through the hands of others. Now I will return the favor as You make me able. I choose to develop philanthropy and to be a trustworthy steward of all You give. I'll be a bank for You here on earth so that others can draw from Your goodness and grace.

SIMPLE TRUTH

Philanthropists are not always wealthy—just generous.

CONFIDENCE

Though a host encamp against me, my heart shall not fear;
though war arise against me, yet I will be confident.

PSALM 27:3 RSV

FROM THE FATHER'S HEART

My child, where do you really place your trust? In your
strength? In your knowledge? In your education? In your
appearance or status? Those things will ultimately fail. Real
confidence will come when you keep your eyes on Me,
trusting Me to guard you from any harmful thoughts, patterns of behavior, or circumstances. The name of Jesus—and
no other—is your true confidence. Trust Me completely.

FROM A SEEKING HEART

Lord, in the past, I have looked in so many directions for the
confidence I needed. Mustering my own self-efforts ends in
failure, but acknowledging You brings success. When I let
You pinpoint the source of my failures and search my heart,
You always show me the problem. You tear down the barriers, excuse by excuse, remove the fears and doubts, and grant
confidence. I speak Your name often, Lord, and choose confidence—believing what You say is true.

SIMPLE TRUTH

It's using His name, not ours, that gives us authority.

WEAKNESS

*But he said to me, "My grace is sufficient for you,
for my power is made perfect in weakness."*

2 CORINTHIANS 12:9

FROM THE FATHER'S HEART

My child, do you feel weak? Unable to go on in your own strength? Don't you know I have been waiting for that confession? Weakness becomes a positive quality when it makes you recognize your need for My power in your life. When you admit your powerlessness without Me, I delight in using that very weakness to make your witness and influence strong in another's life.

FROM A SEEKING HEART

Lord, You have humbled me repeatedly, and my pride is bruised from falling. Additional responsibility You've entrusted to me has only reinforced my weakness. Yet I'm beginning to see that true weakness is not relying on the flesh; it's declaring my dependency on You. When I am weak, You are strong. Strange, but the very times I've felt most inadequate and reached out to You are the times when I've felt most effective. Lord, truly I am powerless without You.

SIMPLE TRUTH

Only God could delight in powerful weakness.

MELODIOUSNESS

He put a new song in my mouth, a hymn of praise to our God.

PSALM 40:3

FROM THE FATHER'S HEART

My child, if you tried to remove the black notes from the piano keys, you would hinder the instrument's musical possibilities. Likewise, melodiousness comes when you allow Me to bring harmony and melody in your life through positive and negative experiences. As you respond to life's challenges with faith and a teachable spirit, I can touch others with the music of your life and create a hunger for My sweet song of salvation.

FROM A SEEKING HEART

Father, only You could write a melody out of nothing but a few minor notes. I look at life—my own and others—and see only a score of scribbled notes and jumbled lives. But then You open my ears to heaven's music, and I hear the faint strains of a great melody. I am shocked to find that the music is coming from my own heart! Lord, You have put a new song in my heart and in my mouth. Let the melodiousness of Your sweet Spirit in me draw others to know You!

SIMPLE TRUTH

A song is what remains in our hearts when all the instruments are silent.

SERVANT SPIRIT

But he that is greatest among you shall be your servant.

MATTHEW 23:11 KJV

FROM THE FATHER'S HEART

My child, it does not matter if all others overlook your talents and achievements. I see your work. And when you do it for Me, that's what counts. I am more interested in developing a servant spirit in you—the willingness to remain in My Master Potter hands in order to be usable. I want you to serve Me cheerfully, without the need for recognition or honor, so you can help others attain My plan for their lives.

FROM A SEEKING HEART

Lord, we spend too much energy reaching for crowns instead of towels. Your name deserves the honor; Your work deserves our time. You were the perfect example of a servant spirit, Lord—always giving, always serving, always honoring Your heavenly Father. Like Peter, Lord, I feel in need of not just a foot washing but a whole bath! And then allow me the privilege of washing others' feet as I share You joyfully.

SIMPLE TRUTH

Some enter a room and declare, "Here I am!" Others cry joyfully, "There you are!"

ORGANIZATION

"When one rules justly over men, ruling in the fear of God,
he dawns on them like the morning light."

2 SAMUEL 23:3–4 RSV

FROM THE FATHER'S HEART

My child, whether your service is giving orders or dispensing water at the back of the line, organization is not an option. I have created everything in an orderly fashion, and I have given you the tools for organization—everything you need to help you effectively lead others in ministry. As you follow My wisdom and direction, you can look ahead to the completion of a task and involve others in meaningful work.

FROM A SEEKING HEART

Father, being a leader—or even an organized follower—is not always easy. At times, when different problems need ready solutions, I feel inept. My left and right brain get confused over which one is in charge. Lord, today I am abandoning all excuses and saying yes to You. But I need Your help, Lord. With Your guidance, I can use organization to effectively accomplish Your work. Even though I cannot, You can, Lord!

SIMPLE TRUTH

Organization means finding a place for everything—
and putting God in first place.

RESPONSIVENESS

"Go and make disciples of all nations, baptizing them in the name of the Father and of the Son and of the Holy Spirit, and teaching them to obey everything I have commanded you."

MATTHEW 28:19–20

FROM THE FATHER'S HEART

My child, I don't expect you to have all of life's answers. And you don't need a road map other than My Word. But I do expect your responsiveness—following Me in obedience wherever I lead and continuing the work that I started on earth. The harvest is waiting. I need all My children to respond. I will prepare your heart and make you sensitive to My Spirit when you put Me first in your life. Then you can truly make disciples for Me.

FROM A SEEKING HEART

Lord, the thought of continuing the work You started—or of even doing greater works—fills me with a mixture of fear and amazement. I don't know where You're leading me, but I don't need to know. I just need to know You! I choose to follow You, Lord, and to be responsive when Your Spirit tugs at my heart, saying, "Turn here." And nothing would give me greater pleasure than to reproduce disciples for You.

SIMPLE TRUTH

In God's math, one times one never equals just one.

CONCENTRATION

I meditate on your precepts and consider your ways. . . .
I will not neglect your word.

PSALM 119:15–16

FROM THE FATHER'S HEART

My child, I love it when you set aside all other distractions and seek My face. That's when I know you are developing concentration. When you apply My principles to your life, I will give you even more knowledge—and the wisdom to use that understanding each day. Many will never uncover these rare nuggets of truth because they have never learned to concentrate on knowing Me and My ways.

FROM A SEEKING HEART

Father, what is of more importance than hearing Your heart? What other loves try to steal my affections from You? These are the questions I ask when I am tempted to let distractions pull me from my concentration on You. Loving You, completing Your purpose for my life, loving those under my care, knowing and doing what honors You, sharing Your words with those who need to hear—these are the goals I wish to pursue, Lord.

SIMPLE TRUTH

When it's all said and done, what really matters most?

STABILITY

I have set the LORD always before me:
because he is at my right hand, I shall not be moved.

PSALM 16:8 KJV

FROM THE FATHER'S HEART

My child, would you like to know the secret of the hind—
the mountain deer that walks on heights without stumbling? Then set your heart on Me and stay in My presence
daily, and I will give you that kind of stability. With hinds'
feet, you can scale the heights and descend the depths.
When adversity comes, you can trust Me to bring peace and
calm to your life.

FROM A SEEKING HEART

Father, with You beside me, there is no mountain too high
and no valley too deep. Even when everything is shaking
around me like an exploding volcano, Your right hand
reaches out to steady me. Lord, it is my joy to start each day
with You and commit each moment into Your control.
Thank You for the stability You are giving me, Lord.

SIMPLE TRUTH

When you've climbed so high that your body is tired,
Jesus walks in and says, "Child, let's go higher!"

AUTHENTICITY

But whoso keepeth his word,
in him verily is the love of God perfected.

1 JOHN 2:5 KJV

FROM THE FATHER'S HEART

My child, run from the very thought of hypocrisy. Someone is always watching you to see if you really belong to Me. Be who I created you to be. When your actions validate the claims of Christ, I will give you authenticity. Although your relationship with Me does not depend on your performance, your influence with others is greatly affected; therefore, obey My Word with enthusiasm.

FROM A SEEKING HEART

Lord, You were the only One on earth who ever modeled true authenticity. Sometimes the gap between who I really am and what I actually do is so great, I try to shrink back with defeat. Yet You remember that I am dust. You know my heart wants to please You, and You never stop working on my character to give me authenticity. I love Your Word, Lord, and I long to live it out in truth and obedience. Let Your genuine love grow in me until it pushes out every ungodly thought or action. I want to be an authentic Christian.

SIMPLE TRUTH

Authentic Christians have nothing to hide.

MIGHT

Strengthened with all might,
according to his glorious power. . .

COLOSSIANS 1:11 KJV

FROM THE FATHER'S HEART

My child, your strength will fade if you try to play "Super-person" on your own. Instead, let Me be your supernatural strength and develop might in you to accomplish supernatural tasks. Might does not depend on power-driven workouts and well-built muscles; it comes as you exchange your weakness for My strength. Only then will you experience superpower.

FROM A SEEKING HEART

Father, truly I am weak, but You are strong. I know the inner strength You give me is forged from testing my faith and resting all my weight upon Your shoulders. Sagging muscles and weak flesh will accomplish nothing. But Your might—Your inner strength at work in me—can move mountains, Lord. You are a Mighty God!

SIMPLE TRUTH

We often measure strength by greatness. God measures
strength by weakness.

SERENITY

*One of those days Jesus went out to a mountainside to pray,
and spent the night praying to God.*

LUKE 6:12

FROM THE FATHER'S HEART

My child, I love spending time with you. You were created to
have fellowship with Me. The more we are together, the more
you will develop serenity—that quiet assurance that you and
I are intimately acquainted, the best of friends. As you spend
time alone with Me, I will fill your heart with peace and satisfaction. You will find no better Friend than I am.

FROM A SEEKING HEART

Lord, each morning I face a choice: to struggle through a
world of chaos that a barrage of media shoves my way or
to rest in the unchanging love and peace of my heavenly
Father. Some would call the first reality. However, faith-
filled reality is holding on to the serenity of knowing God
is in control. Each day, Lord, I choose the serenity You
offer and will meet You faithfully to start the day and nurture our relationship.

SIMPLE TRUTH

Time with God is the breakfast of true champions.

SINGULARITY

*"But only one thing is needed. Mary has chosen what is better,
and it will not be taken away from her."*

LUKE 10:42

FROM THE FATHER'S HEART

My child, flash back to the time when you didn't know
Me—to the time when every pursuit of your heart fed your
own selfish desires. Is that what you want today? Neither is
that My desire for you. I have greater things planned for
you. Let Me give you singularity so you will choose only
those quests that strengthen your relationship with Me.
Other priorities cry for your attention, but I want your sin-
gular heart's devotion.

FROM A SEEKING HEART

Lord, when I take the time to kneel at Your feet and listen—
really listen—I can hear Your heart so clearly. Worries fade,
and accusations I've made fall foolishly among my tears of re-
pentance. You are all I need. And when I do listen carefully,
I can sense Your heart beating passionately for others. So
great is Your love—so great was Your singularity on earth. I
will devote myself with singularity also, Lord. May my heart
beat as one with Yours.

SIMPLE TRUTH

Love cares more about the people than the preparations.

HARMONY

But if we walk in the light, as he is in the light,
we have fellowship one with another.

1 JOHN 1:7 KJV

FROM THE FATHER'S HEART

My child, I love the music of My children's laughter as they
work together for Me. When I write the notes, they create
a symphony that brings Me great pleasure. That happens as
I give you harmony, the ability to fellowship with others because of My bond of love. When you choose to let Me love
through you, I will make you a true chord of blessing to others. Let the music never end!

FROM A SEEKING HEART

Lord, what a challenge to maintain fellowship with so many
different personalities and gifts! You created us all different,
each with the stamp of "original" on our blueprints. It takes a
variety of notes to make a beautiful melody, but the song only
resonates with harmony when the conductor writes the music.
Lord, I choose to walk in Your light and use harmony to stay
close to You so my fellowship with You—and others—stays
sweet.

SIMPLE TRUTH

Without harmony, life leads to dis-"chord"-ance.

TEACHABILITY

Let the wise listen and add to their learning,
and let the discerning get guidance.

PROVERBS 1:5

FROM THE FATHER'S HEART

My child, keep your mind closed only to those who would feed you harmful information. Although it is My Spirit that gives you true wisdom, teachability understands the value of listening to the godly servants I have placed around you. Teachability keeps your spirit open to weigh the thoughts and opinions of others and helps you choose to approach life as a student and learner under My tuition.

FROM A SEEKING HEART

Father, I can avoid so many mistakes if I will just learn to listen. Boasting in my own knowledge or trying to pretend I know all the answers only makes my ignorance more visible. Lord, I choose teachability. I know so little, but I crave to know You so deeply. I will not choose ungodly advice, but I will surround myself with others who know Your heart and Your Word—so that together we can share Your truths lovingly with everyone. Most of all, I choose You as my Master Teacher.

SIMPLE TRUTH

Practice saying the following words often: "You may be right."

STEADINESS

Teach me your way, O LORD,
and lead me on a level path because of my enemies.

PSALM 27:11 NRSV

FROM THE FATHER'S HEART

My child, just as small children need assistance to keep their "toddling" feet from falling, you need My help, too. Whether you are walking on high mountains, over steep cliffs, or in deep valleys, I will give you steadiness when you keep your eyes on Me. I will place your feet on the right path and direct you until you have reached your destination safely.

FROM A SEEKING HEART

Father, I love to view life from the mountaintops, but I don't like the climbing to reach it: Feet falling over slippery rocks, clinging by my fingernails, hands searching for the next crevice and missing it entirely, I fall back into the valley repeatedly. I have so many scratches and scars that sometimes I just want to quit. And then I remember Your example—and Your Word, Lord. I receive Your promise of steadiness—and I will stay on the path You've outlined for me. Where else could I go but to You, Lord?

SIMPLE TRUTH

What I find at the top makes the climb worthwhile.

TEMPERANCE

*A man without self-control is like a city broken
into and left without walls.*

PROVERBS 25:28 RSV

FROM THE FATHER'S HEART

My child, have you ever visited a war zone or seen the deso-
lation of a terrible earthquake? Piles of rubble, crumbling
ruins lie in heaps around once-fortified cities. That's the
picture of a life without My lordship. I will help you keep
temperance in your life so that it is under the control of My
Holy Spirit and in pursuit of peace. I will give you My protection as you yield every impulse and thought to Me.

FROM A SEEKING HEART

Lord, You are the One who keeps the walls of my heart
sound and under control. You prevent the foundation from
crumbling and protect me from every attack. I will not surrender my life to impulses that could destroy my character,
my home, or my family. I will allow nothing or no one to
control me except You. I choose a life of temperance, Lord.
Keep my walls strong!

SIMPLE TRUTH

Never take time to vote on temptation. Just say no.

COMPASSION

Be sympathetic, love as brothers,
be compassionate and humble.

1 PETER 3:8

FROM THE FATHER'S HEART

My child, once you have walked through the fire, you will better understand the burning wounds of another's heart. Throughout your life, I am developing compassion in you by allowing you to experience hurt—so you can see the needs of others through My eyes of love. When others have concerns, needs, or losses, you can feel deeply for them and offer your encouragement, love, and prayers—and point them to Me.

FROM A SEEKING HEART

Lord, every person You touched on earth could share a witness of Your genuine compassion. Tender eyes, extended hands, gentle touch—I can see You now as You brought dignity to the wretched, hope to the destitute, and life to the dying. In fact, Your compassion in my own life moves me to wrap my arms around others and whisper, "God loves you—and so do I!" Lord, because of Your tenderness to me, I must pass compassion on to others!

SIMPLE TRUTH

Sometimes a hug is enough.

EXHILARATION

*Though you have not seen him, you love him; and. . .you believe
in him and are filled with an inexpressible and glorious joy.*

1 PETER 1:8

FROM THE FATHER'S HEART

My child, My love for you has no boundaries. Your birth—
and your life—are a source of joy to Me, and I long for you
to share that joy. As you realize the magnitude of My love
for you, I love it when you can respond like David and Mary
did—with exhilaration—an overwhelming feeling of gratitude and praise. When My Spirit witnesses with your spirit,
I will fill your heart with inexpressible joy.

FROM A SEEKING HEART

Lord, just the very thought of Your love and faithfulness sets
my heart and feet to dancing. I cannot be silent. With hands
lifted and heart bowed, my heart sees what my eyes cannot,
and a sense of exhilaration and anticipation takes over. Lord,
may I never forget the price You paid and the love You gave
for me. With childlike wonder, I choose to awake each day
eager to please and filled with a desire to touch Your heart
with my expressions of love.

SIMPLE TRUTH

*Pray frequently, "Lord, today I ask not what You will
do for me, but what can I do for You?"*

TRUST

Do not be anxious about anything,
but in everything, by prayer and petition,
with thanksgiving, present your requests to God.

PHILIPPIANS 4:6

FROM THE FATHER'S HEART

My child, I am not ignorant of your plight. I never sleep. And
I created you, remember? Have I ever failed to keep one
promise? I know the desires of your heart and life. You can
come to Me with boldness, trusting Me to provide everything
you need. Refuse to worry or fret about the question marks or
apparent injustices in your life. Don't look around anxiously;
look to Me.

FROM A SEEKING HEART

Father, each year bears witness to another season of Your
faithfulness. There is not a need You have not provided; not a
promise has gone unfulfilled. I remember the times I've fret-
ted so foolishly, only to realize I should have trusted You all
along. Today I will exercise my faith in You by reaffirming the
trust You've placed in my heart. For every physical, emotional,
and spiritual need I have, I will turn to You confidently and
boldly, thanking You ahead of time for however You answer.

SIMPLE TRUTH

Worry less—trust more.

RESONANCE

I pray that you, being rooted and established in love, may have power, together with all the saints, to grasp how wide and long and high and deep is the love of Christ. . .that you may be filled to the measure of all the fullness of God.

EPHESIANS 3:17–19

FROM THE FATHER'S HEART

My child, when you feed on My Word, make sure you let its truths soak deeply into your spirit. As you root your heart deeply in My love, I will fill you with its resonance and an acute awareness of all I have done for you. This will result in continuing growth, service, and praise to Me. I want you to grasp the fullness of who I really am—and how much I really love you.

FROM A SEEKING HEART

Father, I want to know You—to really know Your fullness and the depth of all You are. I don't want to be like a shallow plant that withers in the hot sun. Lord, I choose to soak myself in Your Word—and Your love—until Your Spirit overflows. Fill me with Your resonance, Lord. May the fruits of Your Spirit—love, joy, peace, patience, kindness, goodness, faithfulness, gentleness, self-control—reign in my life so that all that You are is all that I want.

SIMPLE TRUTH

To receive His filling, we must first be willing.

FORTITUDE

But now I urge you to keep up your courage.

ACTS 27:22

FROM THE FATHER'S HEART

My child, what you see is not always reality. I often use difficulty and trials as disguised blessings to help build character
in your life. I will give you fortitude—an ability to see reality
with faith-colored glasses. Then you can rely daily on the
inner strength I give to you, keeping on track even when the
circumstances may be unfavorable.

FROM A SEEKING HEART

Father, when I'm up against a wall and feel totally alone,
even then I find Your presence near. Open my eyes that I
might see Your hand at work; open my heart that I might
stay fortified with Your courage. Then open my arms that I
might embrace others with Your encouragement, letting
them know that with You they can walk through anything.

SIMPLE TRUTH
Fortitude requires a faith attitude.

EAGERNESS

Now finish the work, so that your eager willingness
to do it may be matched by your completion of it,
according to your means.

2 CORINTHIANS 8:11

FROM THE FATHER'S HEART

My child, I love to see eagerness in your spirit—a desire to see My work accomplished in whatever way I choose. I have placed you in a strategic position so others might catch the joy and enthusiasm of your heart and join My work. When you make yourself available with enthusiasm, you can influence others to work together for the cause of Christ, too. That makes Me excited as well!

FROM A SEEKING HEART

Father, if eagerness can make up for lack of ability, I am Your servant. I may not have much to give, but I am excited about Your assignment. When I read in Your Word how You used ordinary men and women like me to change the course of history, I'm amazed—and eager to see Your plans unfold for my life. Lord, I am eager to accomplish whatever You want me to do, as a cheerleader or an action player. Send me today, Lord!

SIMPLE TRUTH
Live for the joy of loving Jesus.

RESOLUTION

My heart is steadfast, O God, my heart is steadfast;
I will sing and make music.

PSALM 57:7

FROM THE FATHER'S HEART

My child, I have given you everything you need to live your life for Me and in Me. My Spirit lives in you and will work within you to conform you to My image. But you must choose daily to act upon what I have given you. You must use resolution, the determination to keep your heart and life tuned to Me and the desire to worship Me alone and make My ways known. I will take your willingness and fill your heart with praise.

FROM A SEEKING HEART

Lord, You set Your heart like flint to withstand the pressures You would endure as You walked on earth. You needed no excuses—because You alone had all the answers. With steely trust in Your Father's wisdom, You exemplified resolution. I, too, Lord, want nothing more than to set my heart on You. May my every thought and motive cry resolutely, "Jesus!" from morning until night. Lord, You are the song of my heart.

SIMPLE TRUTH
"I will" does not mean "maybe."

ORIGINALITY

You knit me together in my mother's womb.

PSALM 139:13

FROM THE FATHER'S HEART

My child, I have given you a set of designer genes all your own; there is no one else like you. Do you know how much I enjoyed creating you? Don't try to copy another's behavior, talents, or looks. Just recognize the uniqueness of My creation and let Me shape you into whatever vessel I desire. As a result, you can touch others in a special way with talents and gifts fashioned by Me. I take great pride in My work. You are a Designer's original, and you are of great worth to Me.

FROM A SEEKING HEART

Father, when I look in the mirror, I see the flaws of my character and appearance and immediately run for cover-ups. Yet, because You love me, I know You are still working on me. I am Your creation, personally designed and intimately loved. I will discard all other standards for my life and act according to the originality for which You created me. I will look to You constantly to work out Your perfect plan in my life. If no one else can take my place, that gives me a responsibility to willingly fulfill my role in Your kingdom.

SIMPLE TRUTH

God has written His signature on every life.

UNSELFISHNESS

"I have been crucified with Christ and I no longer live,
but Christ lives in me."

GALATIANS 2:20

FROM THE FATHER'S HEART

My child, you will learn the meaning of unselfishness when
you are willing to exchange your life for My life. As long as
you are operating out of your old nature, you will never understand My best for you. When you accept My death for
your own and willingly release your old self, I will remove
your selfish desires and give you a new heart for others. But
remember, you must *die* daily—and let Me *live* daily in you!

FROM A SEEKING HEART

Lord, no one stretched my arms on splintered beams of wood.
No one drove spikes into my hands or feet. I heard no thuds
of the hammer or claps of thunder before I died. I was not
there at Your crucifixion. Yet by faith I accept Your death as if
it had been my own—for me. By faith I see my old, sinful nature nailed to that cross. And by faith I see a new life—a new
me—resurrected with You. Each day I will submit to You with
the declaration, "I am alive! Yet not me, but Christ in me!"

SIMPLE TRUTH

God does not require martyrdom, though I may expe-
rience that. But He does require the death of self.

GODLINESS

But godliness with contentment is great gain.

1 TIMOTHY 6:6 KJV

FROM THE FATHER'S HEART

My child, have you learned by now that riches bring no lasting happiness? You will find no shopping carts in heaven; you will take no wallets across the threshold. On this earth, you are most blessed when you have food and clothes on your back. What I really want to give you is godliness—a lifestyle and attitude that seeks Me alone. I will develop godliness in you when you shut out all distractions—including the pursuit of wealth—and concentrate on letting Me live through you. Then you will indeed be rich.

FROM A SEEKING HEART

Father, I know about those futile pursuits, and I have discovered that You are the only thing that really satisfies. I desire that godliness in my life, Lord. My pursuit has changed, and my search is to know You—to pursue love, goodness, faith, endurance, gentleness. . . All the things You are—that's what I want to be. I will resist that temptation to accumulate, and I will plant my roots not in possessions but in You, Lord.

SIMPLE TRUTH

The sweetest possession is the obsession for Christ.

REALISM

In the world ye shall have tribulation: but be of good cheer;
I have overcome the world.

JOHN 16:33 KJV

FROM THE FATHER'S HEART

My child, I don't expect you to live in ivory palaces, untouched by human hands or human hearts. The seasons of life must have their perfect work in the lives of My children. I allow rain to fall on them all. You will learn realism when you face life with eyes wide open—an awareness that you must deal with both good and bad situations. You can acknowledge the reality that life is not perfect, but you can also believe the truth of My encouragement. I will make you an overcomer, as well.

FROM A SEEKING HEART

Father, instead of asking, "Why me?" I should be crying, "Why not me?" I choose realism by accepting that life is not fair. But when it is not, Your goodness shines through even stronger. You will never abandon me. You have stretched out my heart in sorrow and given me the capacity for more joy. You have stilled storms, moved mountains, and pulled me out of deep pits. Through it all, Lord—whatever happens to me— You will make me victorious when I keep my eyes on You.

SIMPLE TRUTH

Whatever comes, we can overcome.

PERSISTENCE

*To those who by persistence in doing good seek glory,
honor and immortality, he will give eternal life.*

ROMANS 2:7

FROM THE FATHER'S HEART

My child, seeking honor for yourself will soon disappoint.
Fame never lasts. Others will forget you, but your name is
written on My hands and heart forever. I will give you persistence when you constantly believe that My kingdom
work matters more than any other endeavor. When you seek
My glory and not your own, I will give you grace to remain
unchangeable in every task I assign. Mothering a child, encouraging a friend, loving the lonely—My kingdom work
may seem small at times, but it's not to me. Keep at it.

FROM A SEEKING HEART

Lord, so many vie for my time and attention. Good things
call—yet I don't see Your name on them. Temptations
come—but making a name for myself gives me no pleasure.
Only making You known matters now. I will always have
choices, and there will always be more work to do than I can
possibly accomplish. But with Your help, I choose persistence
so I can stay at the tasks You assign. Only the ones You choose
for my life will make a difference. Make them plain, Lord.

SIMPLE TRUTH
It matters to God.

GENTLENESS

Brothers, if someone is caught in a sin,
you who are spiritual should restore him gently.

GALATIANS 6:1

FROM THE FATHER'S HEART

My child, it is by My grace and love that you are where you are in life right now. You have no idea how many times My protective hand has kept harm away from you—greater harm than anything you have ever experienced. I want you to exercise the same gentleness as you see from Me—loving others as I have loved you. Gentleness helps you recognize your own potential for sin and puts you in another person's place to better understand and help him or her.

FROM A SEEKING HEART

Lord, how many times you have caught me on the way down or picked me up after a fall! Gently, You've brushed my tears away and set me on solid ground again. I can do no less for another. I choose not to deal harshly with others and to first examine my own life to find any beams lodged there. I will not point fingers, but I will simply point others to You, Lord. In gentleness, I will help them find spiritual restoration.

SIMPLE TRUTH
Gentle ways bring better days.

UPRIGHTNESS

The way of the LORD is strength to the upright.

PROVERBS 10:29 KJV

FROM THE FATHER'S HEART

My child, did you know that your obedience and faithfulness is like a shelter from the cold, harsh winds of destruction? Choosing Me and My ways puts you out in harm's way and in heaven's pathway of blessing! When you are willing to cling to Me and accept My holiness for your own, I will give you uprightness. I will give you a heart sold out to Me and a life of honesty and integrity.

FROM A SEEKING HEART

Lord, nothing good comes from turning aside from Your path for our lives. And we can do nothing good without Your holiness and uprightness—the "rightness with God" You gave us when You died for us and made us Your children. Your uprightness is a gift, and I receive it gladly. I find my strength in You.

SIMPLE TRUTH

God's provision for uprightness is "downright" wonderful.

ANTICIPATION

*Then we which are alive and remain shall be caught up
together with them in the clouds, to meet the Lord in the air.*

1 THESSALONIANS 4:17 KJV

FROM THE FATHER'S HEART

My child, if I allowed you one glimpse of heaven, you would
not hold so tightly to the things here on earth. Instead, you
would grieve because you could not experience it sooner! But
I do not want to give you grief, only anticipation—so you can
live expectantly as if I were coming today. When I open your
eyes to the future hope you have in Me, all other loves will
fade, and you can rejoice and live purposefully for My return.

FROM A SEEKING HEART

Lord, when I think about heaven, I get so excited! Like Paul,
I am torn sometimes. I want to stay here because of the ones
You have given me to love and the work You have assigned me
to do. But I long to see the One for whom my heart beats faster
than any other! I long to see You, Jesus! On some days when
everything falls apart, when pain grows too intense, and when
losses mount too high, I really long for my real home with You.
But in the meantime, I choose to anticipate every day as if it
were my last—and to make each day count for You.

SIMPLE TRUTH
Today is one more day closer to eternity.

PRODUCTIVITY

*Whatever you do, work at it with all your heart,
as working for the Lord, not for men.*

COLOSSIANS 3:23

FROM THE FATHER'S HEART

My child, how do you feel about your assignment? Whether you are hammering a nail, directing a staff, washing a dish, or teaching a class, I will give you productivity—a sense of accomplishment and pride in your work—when you commit your work to Me. When I am your employer, the only reward you need is to know you have been faithful to your task.

FROM A SEEKING HEART

Father, I do not always understand why You place us where you do. And I may not always like the conditions under which I work. But out of gratitude to You for Your endless goodness, faithfulness, and love, I choose to make my work a sacrifice of praise for You alone. It is You who grants me promotion, and it is You I desire to please. It doesn't matter where I serve, Lord. But I will serve You with all my heart.

SIMPLE TRUTH

His smile makes it all worthwhile.

HONESTY

LORD, who may dwell in your sanctuary? . . .
He whose walk is blameless and who does what is righteous,
who speaks the truth from his heart
and has no slander on his tongue. . .

PSALM 15:1–3

FROM THE FATHER'S HEART

My child, secrets not only destroy family unity on earth; they prevent intimacy in your relationship with Me and others. Choose honesty so you can live before Me and others without pretense or secrets. Let your life be an open book of testimony to Me, and remember to treat others with dignity and respect. Isn't that the way you want others to respond to you? Haven't I been honest with you in My Word?

FROM A SEEKING HEART

Lord, You withhold no good thing from Your children; You are honest in all Your dealings with us. We sometimes think hiding will bring relief, but it only causes a simmering earthquake inside that will eventually erupt. Lord, I choose honesty with You and invite You to walk through my heart often, repairing and refurbishing as needed. And I choose to make honesty a way of life so that others can see You clearly.

SIMPLE TRUTH

Integrity is always open for inspection.

FORBEARANCE

*Forbearing one another
and, if one has a complaint against another,
forgiving each other. . .*

COLOSSIANS 3:13 RSV

FROM THE FATHER'S HEART

My child, I want to develop in you a heart like Mine. The world needs to see love in action. You will learn forbearance by extending the same grace and patience to others that I have given you—not because they deserve it—but because they need it. You can actually turn darts of hatred into arrows of love by dealing gently with others. Wear My clothing of love and forbearance daily.

FROM A SEEKING HEART

Father, holding grudges sounds so. . .grungy. Forgive me for the times I *forget* to forgive others, thinking that the offense will simply fade away with time. Lord, I want to take no chances on ruining a relationship. If I offend someone or if someone offends me, I will take action immediately to make sure our relationship is secure and all is forgiven as much as is possible. I will cover others' faults with Your love and choose forbearance.

SIMPLE TRUTH

Forbearance is far better than being a bear.

INVINCIBILITY

Put on the full armor of God.

EPHESIANS 6:11

FROM THE FATHER'S HEART

My child, did you know I have provided designer clothing for you to wear? It's your choice, but the cost has already been paid. When you faithfully wear My armor, trusting in My ability, not yours, I will develop invincibility in you. No matter how great the odds, with My help you can stand strong under the pressures of temptation or difficulties. Remember, your struggle is otherworldly—against wicked spiritual forces. You need My protective clothing.

FROM A SEEKING HEART

Father, I've tried fighting without Your protective armor, and I now choose to wear every piece You've provided: the belt of truth, the breastplate of righteousness, shoes of peace, the helmet of salvation, the shield of faith, and the sword of the Spirit—Your Word dividing clearly truth from fiction. And above all I choose a covering of prayer in Your Spirit, always keeping alert for dangerous schemes and deadly beams of lies aimed at my destruction. Lord, with Your help, I choose invincibility.

SIMPLE TRUTH

Don't forget to cover your Achilles' heel.

LIBERALITY

*How that in a great trial of affliction the abundance of their joy
and their deep poverty abounded unto the riches of their liberality.*

2 CORINTHIANS 8:2 KJV

FROM THE FATHER'S HEART

My child, it pleases Me when from the goodness of their
hearts, My children open their pocketbooks for godly causes.
But when I see the *widows' mite* gift—the one offered from a
heart of true poverty—I know that life is sold out to Me. Liberality comes so you can give sacrificially to others out of your
overwhelming gratitude to Me. Whether you are rich or
poor, you can always find someone who is needier than you.

FROM A SEEKING HEART

Father, no one ever gave more or loved more than You. My
own liberality pales to Your sacrificial love gift—Your own
Son's death by crucifixion for me so I could have a personal
relationship with You! I not only want to give liberally to
those in need when my bank account is full; but, Lord, I want
to trust You to provide something I can give, even when the
balance says zero. I choose liberality as a way of life. How can
I do any less?

SIMPLE TRUTH

*Becoming a liberal channel of blessing does not require
money.*

WATCHFULNESS

O LORD, in the morning thou dost hear my voice;
in the morning I prepare a sacrifice for thee, and watch.

PSALM 5:3 RSV

FROM THE FATHER'S HEART

My child, your hungry body needs the proper nutrition at
the start of your day or you will burn out quickly. In the
same way, you must take time for spiritual nourishment to
face the demands you'll encounter. I will develop watchful-
ness in you as you eagerly wait for My voice. Determine to
meet Me daily, and trust Me to fill your hungry heart and
open hands with My plans for your day. Don't leave home
without Me.

FROM A SEEKING HEART

Father, neglecting You and Your Word usually results in
spiritual malnutrition and dehydration. I am helpless without You! Starting the day without You and without my spiritual armor is like facing a battlefield. I must be prepared,
Lord! With Your help, I will meet You daily, hungry to be
fed, thirsty for more of You, and watchful of every opportunity to live positively for You.

SIMPLE TRUTH

If we listen well the first time, God will not have to
teach us the same lessons repeatedly.

MANAGEMENT

Thou hast given him dominion over the works of thy hands.

PSALM 8:6 RSV

FROM THE FATHER'S HEART

My child, when I gave man dominion over the earth, it was not because the world was too big for Me. I could have managed it without your help. But I chose to give you responsibility and allow you to share in the joy of My creation. I am developing in you the quality of management, the ability to handle wisely the responsibilities I have given you. Wherever I place you, you can exercise good judgment in taking care of My creation.

FROM A SEEKING HEART

Father, what an awesome task we have as Your children to care for Your creation. Forgive us when we plunder instead of protect; when we rob instead of restore; when we waste instead of preserve. I will do my part in little and big ways and accept the responsibility of management. I am only one, but I am one who believes in making a difference. I will honor the beauty and magnificence of the world You created—and in doing so, I will be honoring You.

SIMPLE TRUTH

If we do not manage well what we have been given, there will be nothing left to manage.

BALANCE

"But seek first his kingdom and his righteousness,
and all these things will be given to you as well."

Matthew 6:33

From the Father's Heart

My child, how many activities have you added to your schedule this year? In how many of those did you consult Me for wisdom? My plan for you has always been balance, letting Me order your life the way I want. Balance helps you keep a right perspective, cutting out the clutter and concentrating on the most important things of life. When other things seek you out, make sure you seek Me first—and then decide.

From a Seeking Heart

Lord, Your perfectly balanced life challenges me to think before I act or speak. Even though I have cried no to every harmful activity that would steal my affections from You, I must gain balance over my thought life as well. Lord, seeking You first means no one else gets more priority than You. My affection, my time, my energy for You is at the top of the day's list. I need You to keep me balanced. I've never been good at juggling.

Simple Truth

The things we choose are a reflection of the qualities
we admire.

IMAGINATION

"No eye has seen, no ear has heard, no mind has conceived what God has prepared for those who love him."

1 CORINTHIANS 2:9

FROM THE FATHER'S HEART

My child, long before you were born, I visualized great things for you. Your life may be dotted with disappointments and failures, but I can work all those things together for My good and help you finish well. Let Me give you imagination so you can visualize Me at work in your life and in the hearts of others. Give Me freedom to speak to you, and guard carefully those things you watch and read. Allow My Spirit full reign in your life.

FROM A SEEKING HEART

Father, each time I study Your creation, the intricacies, the uniqueness of each created thing, I am amazed at Your imagination. I have no conception of Your detailed plans for my life, but I know You are working for my good. I will think on things that are good, helpful, positive, and worthwhile—and I will use the mind of Christ You've given me to visualize impossible things that only You can do. And I will keep a clean vessel so Your message and Your plan will not be obscured by sin.

SIMPLE TRUTH

What God can conceive, God will achieve.

ATTENTIVENESS

*Be sure you know the condition of your flocks,
give careful attention to your herds.*

PROVERBS 27:23

FROM THE FATHER'S HEART

My child, no one lives to himself. I have planned for all My children to care for and be cared for by another. I will give you attentiveness to keep your eyes and ears open to My world so that I can use you at a moment's notice. Then you can tune in to My leadership and make yourself intentionally available to those I have entrusted to your care. Keep spiritually alert. Others need your protection.

FROM A SEEKING HEART

Father, nothing happens to us that escapes Your attention. You know the number of hairs on our heads—certainly You pay attention to our needs. I, too, want to exercise attentiveness, Lord. I will take every precaution to protect those You have placed under my care. I understand that "two are better than one" and that having an important part in Your kingdom work is a privilege and a responsibility.

SIMPLE TRUTH

Never leave your "flock" without a covering of prayer.

APTITUDE

God's gifts and his call are irrevocable.

ROMANS 11:29

FROM THE FATHER'S HEART

My child, once I chose to open the door of salvation to everyone regardless of their race, that "call" could not be changed. Whether Gentile or Jew, the only condition by which one becomes My true child in the kingdom is to turn from sin and accept My invitation: the death and resurrection of Jesus as payment for sin. Likewise, I give all My children gifts. Aptitude is choosing to make exceptional use of those gifts I have given you. Agree with Me that your life and talents can make a difference—when submitted to My touch.

FROM A SEEKING HEART

Father, I do not covet others' gifts. I only want to use the ones I have to honor You. Forgive me for the times I've wasted opportunities, questioned Your gifts, or misunderstood their purpose. Whatever time You've allowed for me, whether short or long, I will use it wisely and develop well Your precious gifts to me. With Your help, Lord, may I make a difference for You?

SIMPLE TRUTH

Your "I will" is more important than the skill.

INDUSTRIOUSNESS

*Work with your hands. . .so that you will not
be dependent on anybody.*

1 THESSALONIANS 4:11–12

FROM THE FATHER'S HEART

My child, when you arise each day, think of your work as a
gift to share and a privilege to enjoy. When others see you
enjoying work that matters—and every good work matters
to Me—you will be honoring Me. Work enthusiastically
because I am your real employer. As you willingly place your
life at My disposal, I will energize you to accomplish your
work with dignity and pride.

FROM A SEEKING HEART

Lord, even as the Son of God, You worked with Your own
hands as a carpenter, developing a trade that would bless others and help Your earthly father. When Your time of ministry
arrived, Your hands blessed, healed, comforted, encouraged,
touched, and loved. With the industriousness of Your own
hands and the incredible love of Your Father's heart, You
turned the world upside down. Lord, with Your help, I will
work diligently and let industriousness characterize my work
for You.

SIMPLE TRUTH

*There's nothing more rewarding than a job well done
in a job well loved.*

CONTRITION

The sacrifice acceptable to God is a broken spirit;
a broken and contrite heart, O God, thou wilt not despise.

PSALM 51:17 RSV

FROM THE FATHER'S HEART

My child, it's not the things you *do* for Me that please Me the most. It's not the sacrifices of time or energy but contrition that I desire in you—the realization that your own sin breaks My heart. Never allow your heart to crust over with disobedience. When you grieve over the same things that grieve Me and let Me turn your life in a new direction, your broken heart becomes an acceptable sacrifice to Me.

FROM A SEEKING HEART

Father, I have broken Your heart so many times with the sin in my own life that I now grieve over the very thought of dishonoring You. Thank You for taking me at my worst, for allowing me to be broken, and for showing me how sin separates me from Your fellowship. I do offer You contrition, Lord. I want nothing more than to live a life pleasing to You. I hate doing wrong, and I choose to do right.

SIMPLE TRUTH

Brokenness is seeing sin the same way God does.

MERCY

"Blessed are the merciful, for they will be shown mercy."

MATTHEW 5:7

FROM THE FATHER'S HEART

My child, close your eyes and remember for a moment. What was your life like before you came to know Me? How have I shown you mercy? You learn mercy as you extend My love toward another. Recognize that I have not given you what you deserve, but with My blood, I chose to clear your account. Because of My gift, can you do any less than forgive and love others as well?

FROM A SEEKING HEART

Lord, there is nothing good enough in me to deserve Your mercy. You offered pure love, a costly sacrifice I could never repay. Time and again, You have held up my account and stamped *forgiven* on each page. You served my eternal death sentence—then set me free. Because of the mercy You extended to me, I will offer that same mercy to those around me, even when that mercy is not deserved.

SIMPLE TRUTH

Mercy recognizes that worth comes from God, not from our works.

POWER

"But you will receive power when the Holy Spirit comes on you;
and you will be my witnesses. . .to the ends of the earth."

ACTS 1:8

FROM THE FATHER'S HEART

My child, many feel powerless because they think they have
not gained enough wisdom or wealth. None of them truly
understands My power and what it's for. I will give you
power and boldness to live and testify for Me as you wait
before Me patiently. When you yield your life to Me, asking for My cleansing and forgiveness, you can then be
plugged into My power source, the Holy Spirit.

FROM A SEEKING HEART

Lord, the times I have felt powerless are the times when I've
neglected discipline in my life, when I've depended on my
own strength, or when I have allowed others or other things
to control me. I don't want to live in timidity or weakness.
So much waits to be done, and so many need to be told
about You. However You choose to do that through me is
fine, Lord, but I choose to wait on You, believing that the
Holy Spirit will fill me with the power I need.

SIMPLE TRUTH

With His Spirit, we have power for every hour.

PRACTICALITY

Pure religion. . .is this, To visit the fatherless and widows in their affliction, and to keep himself unspotted from the world.

JAMES 1:27 KJV

FROM THE FATHER'S HEART

My child, flashy words and famous works do not pull My heartstrings. What I love most is a heart surrendered to do a servant's job. Let me give you practicality so you can live Christianity in a way that touches others profoundly, simply, and quickly. Learn to pattern your life after Mine, doing good everywhere you go—whether anyone notices or not.

FROM A SEEKING HEART

Lord, in Your Word I see You walking by the sea, sitting on a mountaintop, stopping by a village, teaching in the temple—always taking time to touch a child, heal a leper, visit the lonely, free the imprisoned, and encourage the weak. Good flowed constantly from You like the ocean tide. We strive for lofty goals and often miss the most obvious opportunities to share Your love. Father, I choose practicality—and with Your help, to see people through Your eyes, allowing pure and simple goodness to punctuate every day.

SIMPLE TRUTH

Every need is an opportunity to show God's love and faithfulness.

PRUDENCE

A prudent man sees danger and takes refuge,
but the simple keep going and suffer for it.

PROVERBS 22:3

FROM THE FATHER'S HEART

My child, pay attention to the rough places in the road and the caution signs I have placed all along your journey. Let Me develop prudence in you so you will have an accurate understanding of right and wrong and the ability to sense danger ahead of time. Take care to hide My Word in your heart, and look to Me to make your eyes keen and your heart pure. By so doing, you will avoid needless disaster and suffering.

FROM A SEEKING HEART

Father, my scars still seem fresh from the falls and wrong choices of my detours. You knew all along what roads would lead to success and which ones would end in failure. From this point on, Lord, I choose to listen to You, to meditate daily on the principles in Your Word, and to hide Your truths so securely in my spirit that I can see the waiting dangers. Lord, give me prudence that I might act wisely every day.

SIMPLE TRUTH

It's never too late to start over.

INTUITION

I will listen to what God the LORD will say.

PSALM 85:8

FROM THE FATHER'S HEART

My child, sometimes you listen, but do you really hear what I am saying? Your thoughts speed ahead like cars on a race-track. Stop often. . .and really listen. When you listen carefully to My Word and to My Spirit within you, refusing to run ahead of Me, I will give you intuition. Then your spirit can agree with Mine, and you can approach life confident that your decisions are pleasing to Me.

FROM A SEEKING HEART

Father, my brain is on a fast track constantly, headed to who knows where? Words follow closely behind, often chasing and overtaking my thoughts—causing me to speak before I think. I'm tired of crashing and burning against walls of fool-ishness. Lord, You've designed maintenance stops all along the route that remind my spirit to slow down and listen. I will exercise that intuition, Lord, and see Your Word—and Your Spirit—as a holy checkpoint to protect my life from self-destruction and early burnout.

SIMPLE TRUTH

Without a good maintenance program, even the best cars may crash and burn.

DISCRETION

*"May the LORD give you discretion and understanding. . .
so that you may keep the law of the LORD your God."*

1 CHRONICLES 22:12

FROM THE FATHER'S HEART

My child, if you are to follow Me and accomplish the tasks
I've assigned you, you must have My discretion and understanding. Halfhearted, thoughtless efforts will not honor
Me and will only bring you discouragement and failure. I
will give you discretion so you will have the ability to use
your head and heart wisely in decision making. Others will
look to you for wisdom. I will help you to apply My Word
for obedient living—but you must keep relying on Me.

FROM A SEEKING HEART

Father, we have all learned painful lessons of acting without
discretion. Thoughtless, selfish deeds only drive people
away from us—and You—not toward You. Radical obedience is my heart's desire—however that shakes out. I choose
to act with discretion, not just when others are watching,
but behind closed doors when only You are my witness.
Thank You for patiently loving me!

SIMPLE TRUTH

Make discretion a permanent possession.

KINDNESS

"The LORD bless you for showing this kindness. . . . May the
LORD now show you kindness and faithfulness, and I too will
show you the same favor because you have done this."

2 SAMUEL 2:5–6

FROM THE FATHER'S HEART

My child, I have always treated you with kindness because
of My great love for you. In the same way, I want you to
mirror that kindness. I want your life to give that silent yet
verbal message from one heart to another that says, "You're
special." Because I have shown you unlimited kindness, you,
too, can treat others with love and goodness—whether they
deserve it or not.

FROM A SEEKING HEART

Lord, if kindness was measured in tangible treasures, I would
be wealthy by now—because of the deposits You have made
in my life. Yet I am—spiritually wealthy. I choose to write
checks on that account daily. With Your help, Lord, may
kindness be a way of life for me as I intentionally relay to
others the constant truth: "You are of great value—you are
loved!" especially when they least expect it.

SIMPLE TRUTH

A kindness showed is a blessing received.

WINSOMENESS

A word aptly spoken is like apples of gold in settings of silver.

PROVERBS 25:11

FROM THE FATHER'S HEART

My child, true beauty is more than what the physical eye can see. But it can be felt—and seen—with the heart and with the spirit. Winsomeness is far more important than your outward appearance. Whether through a wisely chosen word, a kind gesture, or a gracious countenance, I want to develop this quality in you. You can use winsomeness to attract others to the beauty of Christ.

FROM A SEEKING HEART

Father, the hours I spend in front of mirrors are useless if I don't allow You to redo the makeup of my heart. There You will birth positive and wholesome thoughts; there You will form the encouraging nuggets of gold that I can pass on to others; there, in my heart, You light up a smile that stretches all the way to my face. Lord, I choose to receive Your winsomeness—so that others can see the true Light of my life.

SIMPLE TRUTH

Beautiful hearts make beautiful faces.

CONVICTION

"Be strong and very courageous.
Be careful to obey all the law my servant
Moses gave you; do not turn from it to the right or to the left."

JOSHUA 1:7

FROM THE FATHER'S HEART

My child, just like it was with Joshua, let today be moving day for you—the time when you cross over from one side to another. Let Me build strong conviction in you—the belief that My Word is the ultimate authority for your choices in life. As you meditate on My Word daily, I will form those beliefs in your heart that are true, right, and pleasing to Me. Then you will be ready to possess the "land" that I have already given you.

FROM A SEEKING HEART

Father, You have given me the title to the land of victorious living. I want conviction, not preference, to characterize my life. Help me to obey the black-and-white truths in Your Word and to discern the principles behind the gray areas—to know Your heart so well that I can move with faith and determination anytime You say, "Go!" I choose to let You form my convictions, based solely on Scripture, and to walk faithfully the path You have outlined for me—letting Your love be my guide.

SIMPLE TRUTH

Conviction is only preference if we write the rules, not God.

REASONABLENESS

"Come now, let us reason together," says the LORD.

ISAIAH 1:18

FROM THE FATHER'S HEART

My child, I have been patient with you in your weaknesses and have invited you to come to Me often to share your heart. Will you, too, be patient with others? I will develop in you reasonableness as you are willing to listen openly and fairly to the viewpoints and ideas of others and to communicate love without restrictions. As you learn to talk honestly and openly with Me, I will help you value the thoughts of others.

FROM A SEEKING HEART

Father, You have listened to my foolish arguments, corrected my faulty thinking, and loved me in spite of it all. Not only do I want to have the kind of heart that is not defensive with You—that readily admits mistakes and disobedience—but I choose to act with reasonableness as I listen and share with others. You are the only One with infallibility; therefore, I can learn so much from others—just by listening.

SIMPLE TRUTH

Offering a kind word means more than having the last word.

JUSTICE

*To do justice and judgment is more acceptable
to the LORD than sacrifice.*

PROVERBS 21:3 KJV

FROM THE FATHER'S HEART

My child, never let your heart become hardened through dishonesty or revenge. Although justice may seem slow, My timing is always perfect. I take note of every foul intention, and I am always at work to change unrepentant hearts with My loving discipline. I will develop in you a sense of justice—treating others as if you were doing business with Me. As you choose to be fair and honest in your relationships, whether others are or not, you will bring honor to Me as well. Do what is right.

FROM A SEEKING HEART

Lord, I know that justice is more than a ruling handed down by twelve tired jurors and an experienced judge. While every decision may not seem fair to me, I can trust You to bring justice to my life. Regardless of how someone treats me, I choose to conduct my work and my life with honesty and integrity, making sure I do the right thing—according to the principles in Your Word.

SIMPLE TRUTH

*Others may not applaud our right actions, but they
will judge our wrong ones.*

IMPRESSIONABILITY

"I desire to do your will, O my God; your law is within my heart."

PSALM 40:8

FROM THE FATHER'S HEART

My child, when you are young and impressionable, everything is seen through the eyes of a child. Change may come harder with age, along with the heart and its arteries. But when you place your life at My disposal, I can revive that impressionability—allowing you to maintain a heart pliable enough for Me to mold and shape for My glory. As you live daily in My presence, I can place My thumbprint on your life—and others will be drawn to the image of Christ in you. You can still begin again.

FROM A SEEKING HEART

Father, everything around me forms impressions on my heart. I make choices accordingly. But above all, I want the kind of impressionability that changes me from the inside out by You alone. I willingly abandon anything that will give or leave the wrong impression on my life, and I gladly run to You, Lord. I will "write" Your Word on my heart daily as I spend time meditating on the truths of Scripture and discover more and more about who You are.

SIMPLE TRUTH

Never suppress the impression of God's Spirit.

PROMPTNESS

Everyone should be quick to listen,
slow to speak and slow to become angry.

JAMES 1:19

FROM THE FATHER'S HEART

My child, life is fragile, and the minutes tick away your time here on earth daily. Your choices can make a difference in life or death for someone. I want you to develop promptness and live in a spirit of readiness so that you can hear My call on your life daily. When you are listening, My Spirit can easily nudge you to speak, move, or work for Me without delay.

FROM A SEEKING HEART

Father, in the past I have allowed harried schedules, disappointments, or wrong priorities to dull my hearing. Instead of quickly answering Your call with, "Here am I, Lord, speak!" my feet shuffled with weariness and apathy as if to say, "Could it wait until later, Lord?" Others suffer from my thoughtless responses and angry reactions. From now on, I choose promptness and will act immediately on Your Spirit's voice. Line up my life with Your Word so my priorities are without question giving You first place.

SIMPLE TRUTH

Procrastination is a slow assassination of life.

CONSECRATION

*"Consecrate yourselves, for tomorrow
the LORD will do amazing things among you."*

JOSHUA 3:5

FROM THE FATHER'S HEART

My child, those who want to experience My hand of blessing must abide in Me daily, nurturing our relationship.
Choose consecration—living your life cleanly and purely
and dedicated to My glory. It is My hand at work in your
life daily that prepares you for the joys of heaven. I long to
see you come into My presence each day with a spirit eager
to know Me deeply. When you do, I will not disappoint. I
will do amazing things through you.

FROM A SEEKING HEART

Father, what else in life is worth more than being in right
relationship with You? I long to see you do those "amazing
things" but not for show-and-tell. Lord, I want to be a part
of Your miraculous work, being used by You to share Your
love in a hundred different ways. I long to honor You above
all. I choose a life of consecration, but I need Your divine
help to keep my life pure and clean before You and others.

SIMPLE TRUTH

Once-a-week baths never clean adequately.

SOCIABILITY

There is a friend who sticks closer than a brother.

PROVERBS 18:24

FROM THE FATHER'S HEART

My child, people need My love—and people need yours. No matter where you go, you will find people with deep needs just like yourself. Let Me develop sociability in you, the refusal to isolate yourself from others. Accept others as My gift to you. Just as I loved people and spent time with them, you, too, can show friendliness and care about people's needs.

FROM A SEEKING HEART

Lord, it is so easy to walk through life with eyes closed and head bowed, oblivious to the needs of souls around us. We are so programmed by the world to make ourselves number one that we slip into that trap repeatedly. You don't require me to be the life of the party; neither do I want to live like a hermit. What I do want is to mirror Your love to people all around me and to see—really see—them the way You do. Open my eyes and my heart, Lord, and love through me today. Grant me sociability that I may add value to others—and point them to You.

SIMPLE TRUTH

No matter what any of us tries to do, it's always better when there are two.

WILLINGNESS

*"Whatever you have commanded us we will do,
and wherever you send us we will go."*

JOSHUA 1:16

FROM THE FATHER'S HEART

My child, make sure you do not offer Me lip service instead
of heart obedience. I have equipped you with everything
you need for life's battles. Will you trust Me to give you victory? My Spirit will give you willingness so you can give Me
permission to do with your life whatever I choose, whenever
I want. Do I need your permission? No, but I will not force
Myself on anyone—and when you make a choice to follow
and obey Me, regardless of where I lead you—you are proving to Me where your heart really is.

FROM A SEEKING HEART

Lord, a stubborn spirit in me only separates our fellowship—and limits my usefulness. I choose a willing heart,
one that says, "Yes, Lord, yes," to Your commands and to
Your direction. If You leave me to follow my own pursuits,
disaster will result. Just as You willingly obeyed Your heavenly Father in all things, I, too, choose to follow You without question. Teach me Your ways, Lord.

SIMPLE TRUTH

When Jesus calls, just say yes.

CONSCIENTIOUSNESS

I press on to take hold of that for which Christ Jesus took hold of me.

PHILIPPIANS 3:12

FROM THE FATHER'S HEART

My child, there is nothing you can do to earn My favor. You do not have to concentrate on works in order to please Me. If that were true, you would boast of something you did yourself. I have made you pleasing to Me through My own sacrifice; it is a gift to all who will receive it. However, I want My love to compel you to live an active and holy life with conscientiousness—out of gratitude for all I've done for you.

FROM A SEEKING HEART

Lord, like Paul, I want to *know* You and the *power* of Your resurrection. I reject a wimpy faith but choose instead a life of conscientiousness. I know my life will never be completely perfect until the day I stand before You face-to-face in eternity. Failure still follows me with dogged determination, waiting for a handout. But Your Spirit witnesses with my spirit that I belong to You—and I find my soul's longing only in You. Thank You for Your *hold* on me.

SIMPLE TRUTH

There are no stars —only starters who never quit.

OBJECTIVITY

My brothers, as believers in our glorious Lord Jesus Christ,
don't show favoritism.

JAMES 2:1

FROM THE FATHER'S HEART

My child, do you think I dispense gold-covered blessings to
some of My children and nickel-plated ones to others? All
of My children have equal access to the throne room of My
heart. Why, then, do you sometimes withdraw your love
from those you call "unworthy"? I want to give you objectivity so you can truly grant others the right to be themselves. Treat others without partiality, listening and living
through the power of My Spirit.

FROM A SEEKING HEART

Father, I am grateful You did not pass me by when You saw
my "spiritual poverty." I was so clueless before I met You!
You did not call us because of our wealth or status in life or
by how gifted we were. You loved us right where we were.
You saw what we could become in You. Lord, I want Your
objectivity so I can look at others and sincerely treat them
with the love and impartiality You showed to me.

SIMPLE TRUTH
Heaven has only one entrance.

BRIGHTNESS

*"Those who are wise will shine like the brightness
of the heavens, and those who lead many to righteousness,
like the stars for ever and ever."*

Daniel 12:3

From the Father's Heart

My child, there can only be one Star in your life. Brightness
will come into your life when you dim your own lights so
that Mine can shine through you transparently. When you
choose brightness, I know you are willing to be used as a
flame—or as the fuel, whichever will bring the greatest light
and glory to Me. Let Me shine through you today, and others will catch a reflection of My goodness and love.

From a Seeking Heart

Lord, it was You who set the heavens in space and You who
hung the moon. It was You who flung the stars in place and
formed the sun for light. Yet all of Your creations—including me—are only reflectors of the one true Light. You,
Lord, shine brighter than anything. This little light of
mine—Your love that transforms me daily—will shine for
You alone. I choose brightness—but it's You who brings that
light out of hiding.

Simple Truth

His light grows brighter when my light grows dimmer.

ENERGY

But the Lord stood at my side and gave me strength.

2 TIMOTHY 4:17

FROM THE FATHER'S HEART

My child, there will be times when you will feel like everyone has abandoned you. Your strength will be zapped, and you will think you cannot go forward. At those times—and at all times—remember that I will energize you through the power of My Holy Spirit. Even when your spirit is weak, you can reach out to Me and accomplish great things through My strength. I will never leave you.

FROM A SEEKING HEART

Lord, how did You keep going when You ministered such long hours to the multitudes around You? How did You recharge Your human battery? Just as You received power and energy moment by moment from Your heavenly Father, I look to that same source. You are at my side daily, Lord, infusing me with strength. I choose to walk and work not in my own puny weakness but to tap into Your Spirit. There I will find the energy to endure and the power to renew my body, mind, and spirit daily.

SIMPLE TRUTH

His strength will open doors, one at a time.

WARMTH

That their hearts may be encouraged
as they are knit together in love. . .

Colossians 2:2 rsv

From the Father's Heart

My child, people respond to a kind word, a gentle touch, and a sincere smile. Don't you? Let Me fill you with holy warmth as you allow My Spirit to touch others in love through you. Keep the doors of your heart open and welcome to others at all times. By doing so, you may be creating an atmosphere of friendship that will lead to greater opportunities for witness.

From a Seeking Heart

Father, like a child tucked under the covers at night by a caring parent, I feel the nurturing of my relationship with You. You treat us with warmth and tenderness, restoring comfort when we are hurting, for You will not "break a bruised reed" or "snuff out a smoldering wick." I choose in turn to offer warmth to others—many of whom may need to know desperately that someone cares—and that You care, most of all, for them.

Simple Truth
God helps me see a world bigger than myself.

CAPABILITY

*In all these things we are more than conquerors
through him who loved us.*

ROMANS 8:37

FROM THE FATHER'S HEART

My child, why do you question your usefulness? Don't be afraid of the challenges I send your way. Am I not able to meet them all? Have I not equipped you for every situation? I have indeed empowered you to accomplish great things for Me. I have given you capability. Use well the abilities I've chosen for you—great and small—and you will live an overcoming life of faith in My strength.

FROM A SEEKING HEART

Father, I know from past failures that I have no strength to accomplish anything alone. Mountains refuse to move, and seas remain turbulent from weak-kneed faith. I will look to You for supernatural strength—and uncanny capability. While it's true that mountains often crumble one pebble at a time, You are the power behind any change. Thank You for allowing me a part and for equipping me to participate in Your sovereign plans.

SIMPLE TRUTH

His ability gives me capability.

LENIENCE

*"Lord, how many times shall I forgive my brother when
he sins against me?" . . . Jesus answered, "I tell you,
not seven times, but seventy-seven times."*

MATTHEW 18:21–22

FROM THE FATHER'S HEART

My child, do you struggle with unfairness? It's not your job
to call fire down on an offender but to go to him and attempt
restoration. Let Me give you lenience so that you can make
allowance for the faults of others without setting new limitations. Just as I have shown you unconditional mercy and forgiveness, you can choose to extend grace to others as well.

FROM A SEEKING HEART

Lord, how can I forgive others who hurt me so deeply?
How can I offer candy to someone who has just handed me
a poisonous snake? I can't, Lord. But if You will create a
pool of grace and lenience in my heart and let love grow
there; if You will allow me to see a picture of Your forgiveness as You bled out Your life for me; if You will forgive
through me, I know this is possible. I choose lenience over
revenge. And I choose grace over grudges.

SIMPLE TRUTH

*You cannot change a leopard's spots, but God can
change its heart.*

NIMBLENESS

He will make my feet like hinds' feet, and
he will make me to walk upon mine high places.

HABAKKUK 3:19 KJV

FROM THE FATHER'S HEART

My child, you cannot walk along the mountain cliffs or climb the mountain steeps without the proper gear. Too much baggage will weigh you down, and you will lose your footing. I want to develop nimbleness in you, so you will have the ability to walk securely in My strength. No matter where you go, you can move quickly and obediently when empowered by My Spirit.

FROM A SEEKING HEART

Lord, my boots creak and my pack drags the ground as I try to scale heights where I've never gone before. And how can I climb where there are no handholds? Yet I know You will not take me anyplace where You have not already been. I choose to trust You and to walk with nimbleness, one step at a time, knowing that You will give sure footing and inner strength. And together we will enjoy the adventure—and the victory.

SIMPLE TRUTH
Be stable—God is able.

CURIOSITY

"You will. . .find me when you seek me with all your heart."

JEREMIAH 29:13

FROM THE FATHER'S HEART

My child, as long as you live on this earth, you will have questions about Me. When you ask, I will answer, though not always in the way you expect. And when you search, you will indeed find Me waiting to embrace your seeking heart. I have given you curiosity—an open heart in search of a Holy God. You can investigate My promises and claims and indeed find Me willing to answer your questions and needs. Then decide for yourself if what I have promised is true.

FROM A SEEKING HEART

Father, like a curious child, I've come to You with a thousand questions—seeking to know who You are, what You do, how You'll respond, when You'll answer, and what Your plan is for my life. You never shoo me away. You are never too bothered or too busy to listen. Thank You for the curiosity You have given me. I choose to use it to search Your Word, not just for answers but for strength—and most of all, to find You. I not only want to seek You, Lord; I want to *see* You and know You more intimately!

SIMPLE TRUTH

God never turns away an honest seeker.

RECEPTIVITY

*To this you were called, because Christ suffered for you,
leaving you an example, that you should follow in his steps.*

1 PETER 2:21

FROM THE FATHER'S HEART

My child, where you serve Me is not an issue. But *how* you
follow Me is. That may include unfair treatment as others
try to take advantage of you. It may even mean suffering for
My sake. I will develop receptivity in you so that you can
make yourself an open channel of My love in every situation. Watch daily for My activity and move quickly to join
Me in My work whenever I call your name.

FROM A SEEKING HEART

Father, every morning I awake eager to hear Your instructions. Thank You for Your Word and how it speaks daily to
my heart. Wherever You lead me today, I choose to follow
with receptivity, first submitting myself to You. Then whatever comes, I will be ready—and willing—to choose right, to
suffer wrong, to love deeply, and to act quickly at Your call.

SIMPLE TRUTH
Obedience is never an option.

ZEST

*"I have come that they may have life,
and have it to the full."*

JOHN 10:10

FROM THE FATHER'S HEART

My child, as your Good Shepherd, I have provided ample grazing land for you. I protect you, love you, and will allow no enemy to steal you away from My flock. I gave My life for you so you could have life. I have given you zest so you could live life to the fullest. Through Me, you can find joy and purpose and experience a quality of life that is impossible any other way.

FROM A SEEKING HEART

Lord, what a blessing to arise each morning knowing that joy is mine because of You. Life—in all of its fullness—is a gift You have provided daily. I choose to treasure this gift, to use it wisely, and to exercise a zest each day as I live it to full capacity. Nothing else gives me purpose other than knowing You have planned every moment before I was born. You care about my life; therefore, I will not waste a single day!

SIMPLE TRUTH

Zest is living life at its best.

COMPATIBILITY

Make my joy complete by being like-minded,
having the same love, being one in spirit and purpose.

Philippians 2:2

From the Father's Heart

My child, take a moment to count your blessings. Think about what I have done in your life and where you would be without My love. This will help you develop compatibility, for when you realize the grace I've given, you can concentrate on the good in others and share a common bond of love and spirit of unity with My other children. I will bless your relationships with a compatibility that results in joy and peaceful living.

From a Seeking Heart

Father, I may not always agree with others, but I can agree with You. Every person is worth hearing and worth loving. I choose compatibility in my relationships—to see Your potential in others and to concentrate on how all of us as Your children can make a difference. When we are united in one purpose—to love and honor You—there is no limit to what You can do in our lives.

Simple Truth

Compatibility is the ability to come alongside others
without a personal agenda.

DISCERNMENT

*Preserve sound judgment and discernment,
do not let them out of your sight.*

PROVERBS 3:21

FROM THE FATHER'S HEART

My child, do you want to minimize trouble? I have given you
discernment so you can choose cautiously your words and
thoughts—and act wisely in all situations. Using discernment
will not only keep you from stumbling and making foolish
mistakes, but it will even allow your sleep to be sweet and
peaceful. You have My Word and My Spirit to guide you
daily and to give you good judgment. Exercise it often!

FROM A SEEKING HEART

Lord, in all of Your relationships and activities on earth, You
acted with discernment and great wisdom. You preserved
the timing for God's perfect plan by refusing to act selfishly
or hastily. Every word You spoke was bathed in love and
thoughtfulness—yet with great authority. Today I will use
Your gift of discernment and allow Your Spirit to form
every word and guide every step. And I will meditate on
Your Word so it never leaves my mind.

SIMPLE TRUTH

Those who act hastily often fall severely.

PREDICTABILITY

He alone is my rock and my salvation; he is my fortress,
I will never be shaken.

PSALM 62:2

FROM THE FATHER'S HEART

My child, how would others characterize your life? Are your actions and your beliefs predictable? When difficulty comes, do you mumble about your circumstances, crumble under the load, or stumble into My protective arms? A continual, responsive trust in Me will result in a predictability that can withstand outside pressures. As you rely on Me, I will make you strong, steadfast, and unshakable. Isn't that the kind of character you'd like to be known for?

FROM A SEEKING HEART

Father, everywhere I look on the pages of Scripture, I see Your hand at work. And everywhere I look on the pages of my life, I see Your *faithfulness* stamped in bold letters. I choose to leave behind my own patterns of unpredictable faith. How could I do anything but trust You more and more? May I indeed mirror a predictable lifestyle of complete, unshaken faith. With You, Lord, that's my desire, more and more.

SIMPLE TRUTH
Faith wings fly higher.

CHARM

Your beauty should not come from outward adornment. . . .
Instead, it should be that of your inner self,
the unfading beauty of a gentle and quiet spirit.

1 Peter 3:3–4

From the Father's Heart

My child, if you are looking for mirrors to confirm your true charm, you will find they reveal only a partial truth. Designer clothes and expensive jewelry may give the appearance of beauty, but you must look deeper. You will discover charm when you let Me develop a beautiful spirit in you—in tune with My own Spirit. As you dress yourself in the clothes of gentleness and inner strength, I will give you My own reflective beauty.

From a Seeking Heart

Father, I have decided to downsize my budget for outward beauty and increase the value I place on inner qualities. While beauty is enhanced by an attractive frame, it is not Your goal for our lives to develop skin-deep beauty—a charm that can be deceiving. Lord, I want the true charm that comes from Your Spirit's total makeover of my heart: a gentleness and quiet trust that says, "You're in charge, Lord, not me."

Simple Truth

It's not makeup we need but a spiritual makeover.

VIGILANCE

"Be always on the watch, and pray that you may be able to escape all that is about to happen."

LUKE 21:36

FROM THE FATHER'S HEART

My child, the time is coming when you will no longer face choices. Life will cease on this earth, for I am coming again soon to take My children back home to heaven with Me. Let vigilance keep the Holy Spirit as the guard of your heart, always preparing yourself against inevitable battles. Pray diligently. My help and strength are available to fight the enemy. You cannot do it alone.

FROM A SEEKING HEART

Lord, like a soldier who never lets down his guard, I will keep Your Spirit on guard in my heart at all times with vigilance. I look forward to Your coming, and my heart's desire is to be found faithful, not turning aside from the truth and not giving in to weakness. It's only by Your power and might, Lord, that we can stand—but today I make my stand for You!

SIMPLE TRUTH

On your mark, get set, TRUST.

PUNCTUALITY

They received the message with great eagerness.

ACTS 17:11

FROM THE FATHER'S HEART

My child, I want to use you greatly in My kingdom's work. Listen well when I speak. Develop punctuality—the ability to hear and respond quickly to My Spirit's nudges. You will recognize My voice by testing it against Scripture—and by spending time with Me often. Punctuality gives you an eagerness to wait before Me, always ready with, "Here I am, Lord, send me!"

FROM A SEEKING HEART

Father, hearing You speak to me from the pages of Scripture and in the inner parts of my heart makes me wonder why I didn't listen sooner—or longer. Thank You for trusting me with the good news of Your Word, for words of guidance, for comfort in trials, and for correction when I was going astray. I choose punctuality in my hearing—and in my doing, Lord. May I always be quick to obey!

SIMPLE TRUTH
Don't delay! Just obey!

AGGRESSIVENESS

For we cannot but speak the things which we have seen and heard.

ACTS 4:20 KJV

FROM THE FATHER'S HEART

My child, the gospel will be offensive to many, and some may even challenge your allegiance to Me and try to force you to submit to man-made rules. I have transformed your life in a powerful way so you can speak boldly about Me and My life-changing love. Aggressiveness is that positive compulsion to share My message with everyone you can and to make a difference in My world. You are not responsible for the results, only the witness.

FROM A SEEKING HEART

Father, there is a time to speak up and a time to be silent. But the time to be quiet is not when I am sharing the truth about You. Forgive me for the times when I've acted timidly, temporarily forgetting the grace You've shown me when I was far away from You. From this point on, I choose aggressiveness in speaking up for You. Time is short, and Your love compels me to speak up and speak out, whenever and wherever Your Spirit prompts me.

SIMPLE TRUTH

When God writes His message on our hearts, we cannot keep it to ourselves.

SKILLFULNESS

God gave them knowledge and skill in all learning and wisdom.

DANIEL 1:17 KJV

FROM THE FATHER'S HEART

My child, trust Me when I place you in a situation that may seem strange or uncomfortable for you. I will give you skillfulness as you make yourself available and teachable to My truths. As you listen to Me, I will broaden your mind and sharpen your ability to learn and apply My wisdom to your life. Those around you will wonder about your skills—and you will have the opportunity to glorify Me when they discover your skillfulness comes from Me.

FROM A SEEKING HEART

Father, You never call us to a work without preparing us ahead of time. Although there is so much I don't understand, You have made truth clearer to me through Your Word. Every Scripture I have committed to memory; every passage that You've enlightened for me; every difficult circumstance You have brought me through has helped me see that You have been developing skillfulness in me. I do choose to apply those truths and trust that You will work through me no matter where You call me. God, You are awesome!

SIMPLE TRUTH

Even the smallest effort makes a difference.

INITIATIVE

The plans of the diligent lead to profit.

PROVERBS 21:5

FROM THE FATHER'S HEART

My child, taking initiative does not mean moving ahead hastily on your own. Scores of My disciples have tried to act independently of Me—without consulting or waiting on My Spirit. The results have been disastrous and not God-honoring. I will give you initiative—the ability to accomplish My goals without excess prodding—when you listen to My voice rather than the words of others. Obey quickly what I tell you.

FROM A SEEKING HEART

Lord, You knew Your mission and moved quickly but steadily to accomplish it. No one had to remind You of its importance. You acted on Your Father's will with complete initiative. When You speak, Lord, I want to listen—and really hear. Not question, not delay, not think about it and see if Your plans fit into mine. Lord, I will take full responsibility for acting with initiative and radically obeying Your will for my life.

SIMPLE TRUTH

When the Spirit moves, I will, too.

SENSITIVITY

Bear ye one another's burdens, and so fulfil the law of Christ.

GALATIANS 6:2 KJV

FROM THE FATHER'S HEART

My child, do you see what I see? Everywhere I look, there are bowed heads, drooped shoulders, hot tears, and heavy hearts. Let Me fill you with sensitivity so you can feel the hurts and feelings of others in a way that will lighten their load. In a spirit of identification, with My help you can stay tuned to the needs of others and help bear their burdens in love.

FROM A SEEKING HEART

Father, forgive me when demanding schedules, overcommitments, and poor priorities drain my energies and leave me insensitive to the needs of others. Remind me of all the times others have lifted my burdens through a kind word, a loving hug, or a fervent prayer. I choose to turn my priorities over to You, Lord, and to listen to the promptings of Your Spirit. Fill me with sensitivity and a desire to really sense the hurts of others so that together we can take those burdens to You, our great Burden-bearer.

SIMPLE TRUTH
You can be the shoulder someone leans on.

TRUSTWORTHINESS

*"Well done, good and faithful servant! You have been faithful
with a few things; I will put you in charge of many things."*

MATTHEW 25:21

FROM THE FATHER'S HEART

My child, don't hide the talents I've given you. How can I
give you more if you squander the gifts you already have? Accept
faithfully the assignment that is yours. Whether I have
blessed you with little or with much, you can develop trustworthiness
when you handle well the jobs and responsibilities
I give you. Then you can serve Me faithfully and joyfully and
lead others with a desire to please Me. I believe in you.

FROM A SEEKING HEART

Father, thank You for the talents You have given us and for
Your trust in us to multiply those gifts for You. Where I
have failed to invest wisely, forgive me, Lord. I'm choosing
trustworthiness, believing that You will help me channel
those responsibilities and gifts to further Your work. They
are not for my benefit, Lord, though it is a joy to have fulfilling
work. My heart's desire is to hear Your "Well done!"
and to serve You faithfully all my life.

SIMPLE TRUTH

*When God enlarges our opportunities, He will also
enlarge our strength.*

CALMNESS

God is our refuge and strength, an ever-present help in trouble.

PSALM 46:1

FROM THE FATHER'S HEART

My child, how do you respond when there is a whole lot of shaking going on? No matter how severe the tremors or how deep the flood of negative circumstances around you, you need not fear. When your eyes are on Me, I will give you a spirit of calmness—a strong, solid trust and dependency that rests in Me alone. Because I am your refuge, you can live freely and fearlessly, knowing that I am always in control. I will never leave you!

FROM A SEEKING HEART

Lord, You were the epitome of calmness. Harsh winds died, tumultuous seas whimpered, evil spirits fled, and heavy hearts eased at the sound of Your voice. Lord, how can I help others if peace does not reign in my own heart? Today I choose to look not at threatening fears or crippling chaos, but I will fix my eyes on You, Lord. I choose the freedom of calmness—because I know You are always in control. When You are our refuge, worries vanish and peace reigns!

SIMPLE TRUTH

When Jesus speaks to the winds and the seas, the storms in my heart—all worries—cease.

METICULOUSNESS

Do your best to present yourself to God as one approved, a workman who does not need to be ashamed and who correctly handles the word of truth.

2 TIMOTHY 2:15

FROM THE FATHER'S HEART

My child, I have given you the tools you need to discover the truth—and I have provided for you My Son, who is the Truth. Let Me help you develop meticulousness so you can adhere carefully to the principles and truths in My Word without Pharisaic legality. Then you will never be ashamed and can represent Me accurately and sincerely. If you make room for My grace to give balance, My truth will set you and others free.

FROM A SEEKING HEART

Lord, I've tried adhering to rule-keeping. And I've even taught without waiting on Your wisdom and accuracy. But today I choose to prepare my heart well with Your life-giving truth, adding generous portions of grace and forgiveness. Where ignorance still exists, Lord, fill in the details. And where bondage still rules, let freedom ring! Lord, I seek Your approval alone.

SIMPLE TRUTH

Add nothing to His Word but love and truthful application.

VIVACITY

I will greatly rejoice in the LORD,
my soul shall exult in my God.

ISAIAH 61:10 RSV

FROM THE FATHER'S HEART

My child, never lose the thrill of discovery. Approach life not as a spectator but as one who celebrates life to the fullest. Let Me give you vivacity so you can live each day joyfully as a special gift from Me. Vivacity helps you savor the moments I give you with a spirit of thanksgiving by recognizing that all you have comes from My hand. Life is not just what you make it; it's what you let Me make it with you.

FROM A SEEKING HEART

Lord, You not only give life; You are the Way, the Truth, *and* the Life. With You in my life, boredom has no place to hang its shingle. I choose vivacity and acknowledge that the greatest thrill of my life was discovering You. Each morning I will wake the dawn with praise for who You are and with thanks for letting me enjoy another day of intimate relationship with You as Your child.

SIMPLE TRUTH

Life is a celebration in adoration of the One who
gives it to us.

DEFERENCE

Humble yourselves therefore under the mighty hand of God,
that he may exalt you in due time.

1 PETER 5:6 KJV

FROM THE FATHER'S HEART

My child, insisting on being right often reveals hidden pride.
I will teach you deference as you yield to the rights and opinions of others in a spirit of humility. With My help, you can
submit to others without compromising your beliefs. Remember that I demote, and I also exalt. You will find in time
that building My character within you is far more important
than who wins an argument or who receives the honors.

FROM A SEEKING HEART

Lord, what a beautiful example of deference You were. You
listened to others and gave dignity to each person. Yet You
never wavered in Your declaration of truth. You humbled
Yourself, set Your kingly rights aside, and submitted Your
will to Your Father's. No longer will I justify myself, insist
on my rights, or ignore the thoughts of others without a fair
hearing. Lord, I choose deference, and I am submitting my
will to Your will.

SIMPLE TRUTH
> *Opinions can be amended easier than relationships*
> *can be mended.*

GRACIOUSNESS

Dear friend,
you are faithful in what you are doing for the brothers,
even though they are strangers to you.

3 JOHN 5

FROM THE FATHER'S HEART

My child, when you exercise graciousness to others, extending warm love and hospitality, whether they are strangers or friends, you are showing love to Me. In the same way that I have shown you kindness and graciousness, keep sharing My love with the ones I bring into your life. This gives Me great joy and says to others that the gospel is real, practical, and life-changing.

FROM A SEEKING HEART

Father, I cannot count the number of times You've sent an angel in disguise to minister to me. Your faithfulness is like the stars in the heavens—those moments are too numerous to record. Yet I remember Your unfailing graciousness, and I choose to see the people around me in a different light. Lord, let my arms, my hands, my heart, and my lips be messengers of Your love today.

SIMPLE TRUTH

Earth angels may not wear wings, but they are always dressed in heavenly clothes.

PROFICIENCY

He is like a tree. . .which yields its fruit in season and whose leaf does not wither. Whatever he does prospers.

PSALM 1:3

FROM THE FATHER'S HEART

My child, I don't gauge your proficiency by your performance. Proficiency is something I develop in you when you delight in Me and in My Word. Then I will make your efforts profitable according to My plan, not yours. Your idea of success may differ from Mine, but you can rest assured that I know best and will prosper your work in My time. When you live close to the source of life, you cannot help but grow.

FROM A SEEKING HEART

Lord, will we ever learn that success is not defined in human terms like money and accomplishments but by knowing and doing Your will? Lord, I willingly abandon my pursuit of worldly success and agree to a lifelong chase to know You intimately. Like a tree drinking up nourishment through its roots, I will find proficiency—and fruit—by drawing life from You. I am so hungry for You, Lord!

SIMPLE TRUTH

Discovering a green grove of trees in a desert is like finding a growing Christian—you will always discover its Living Water source nearby.

FIRMNESS

Christ is faithful as a son over God's house.
And we are his house,
if we hold on to our courage and the hope of which we boast.

HEBREWS 3:6

FROM THE FATHER'S HEART

My child, you are part of My house. I take great joy and delight in building up that house and enlarging it every time a new believer joins My family. Let Me develop firmness in you, the unshakable quality of conviction that will drive you to obedience. When Christ is your foundation, you can respond to life with courage and strength as a servant of Mine.

FROM A SEEKING HEART

Lord, I don't like walking on shaky ground. Firm up my steps and make the path level where I walk. I am reaffirming my confidence in You, and I am declaring my intention to faithfully carry out the work that You have assigned for me. Thank You for adding on to Your house just to make room for me. My hope, my life, my very courage is centered in You. You are my foundation!

SIMPLE TRUTH

Heaven, our real home, was built to last for eternity.

PERSONALITY

"You crowned him with glory and honor."

HEBREWS 2:7

FROM THE FATHER'S HEART

My child, do you still struggle sometimes with who you are? Don't you know that I have given you a personality of your own patterned after My own and designed especially for Me? If you will adjust to My plans and allow Me to shape you according to My good pleasure, I will use your life in an extraordinary way. Trust Me.

FROM A SEEKING HEART

Lord, we see in ourselves impatient outbursts, obsessive compulsions, mysterious fears, and wimpy hearts—flaws of character we long to change. We marry opposites and cringe at differences—and seem unable to believe that we are uniquely and beautifully made in Your image. When those times come, Lord, You remind me that You are still working on me. Help me see the person I am becoming in You, even though I may feel like I'm taking snail steps. I accept the personality You gave me and will cooperate with You. Because, Lord, more than anything, I really want to be just like You.

SIMPLE TRUTH

To God, we are no mystery—He knows exactly who we'll be.

GIFTEDNESS

We have different gifts, according to the grace given us.

ROMANS 12:6

FROM THE FATHER'S HEART

My child, look around you. Do you see the teacher sur-
rounded by eager students? The teen visiting the nursing
home? The office manager delegating work? The one speaking My truth so clearly? The child praying for a sick friend?
You, too, have giftedness—the awesome and humble awareness that I have allowed you to contribute to My kingdom's
work in multiple ways. As you use those gifts wisely to
encourage, bless, and affirm others, you will be honoring
Me, too.

FROM A SEEKING HEART

Lord, to think that You have gifted me for work in Your
kingdom! What a joy to work for You! I realize I cannot
copy someone else's gift. We are not cookie-cutter replicas
but unique servants equipped just as You designed. With
Your help, I choose to develop my giftedness, Lord, to bless
You and add value to others. I will not compare, envy, or
question. I thank You for the privilege and for the *gift* of
being Your child.

SIMPLE TRUTH

Gifts were given to be opened, used, and enjoyed.

DIPLOMACY

When a man's ways please the LORD,
he makes even his enemies to be at peace with him.

PROVERBS 16:7 RSV

FROM THE FATHER'S HEART

My child, the world is short on diplomacy. Nations will always war against nations, and war will characterize these times from now until I come again. I will give you diplomacy—the art of peacemaking, so you can move gently and wisely between others as My personal representative. When you choose to be at peace with Me, I will use you to help others do the same.

FROM A SEEKING HEART

Lord, even with the fresh smell of gunpowder on the world's breath, I choose to be Your representative and exercise diplomacy. As the supreme Peacemaker, You bridged the gap between God and man and provided a way for war to cease in our hearts. I may not solve the nations' enmities with each other, but I can testify to the One who can. One by one, I can help others fly a personal flag of surrender to You. For You alone bring true peace.

SIMPLE TRUTH

True peace existed long before wars began. And true
peace will reign long after wars cease.

USABILITY

I pray also that the eyes of your heart may be enlightened in order that you may know the hope to which he has called you.

EPHESIANS 1:18

FROM THE FATHER'S HEART

My child, you are like an empty water jar that I long to fill up with Myself. All around you are people hungry and thirsty for Me. They don't know the reason for their emptiness, but I do. I want to give you usability so I can use your life to touch others. When you open yourself to Me and make yourself available, I can fill you up with a new desire to please Me by serving others. Then you can overflow and give others a drink from My Living Water.

FROM A SEEKING HEART

Lord, sometimes I think, *How can You possibly use someone like me?* Then You come and take this weak, unlikely candidate and show me a glimpse of what is possible if I'll only believe. Such grace is beyond my comprehension. Lord, I accept Your promise of usability. Open the eyes of my heart that I may see all You envision and willingly join You in Your work.

SIMPLE TRUTH
Usability depends on His ability—and my availability.

VISIBILITY

For you were once darkness, but now you are light in the Lord.

EPHESIANS 5:8

FROM THE FATHER'S HEART

My child, you cannot see the sun in the blackness of night. And you cannot see My Light in a dark room. Did you forget to turn the Light on in one of the rooms of your heart? I want to give you visibility so you can reflect My true character and Light openly in a dark world. It is not you who shines but My Light shining through you so that others might come to know Me. Your electric bill is paid. Keep the Light on—day and night.

FROM A SEEKING HEART

Lord, how can You be visible, yet invisible? Your Light shone clearly on earth. Some questioned the origin of that Light, but everything about You pointed to Your Father. Lord, I never want to return to darkness. I've been there and done that—but You burned the T-shirt that said so! Now I choose visibility. You are my Light! You have freed me from the darkness of a sinful heart. I want others to see that Light and find freedom, too.

SIMPLE TRUTH

Those who choose to live in darkness have never really seen the Light.

JUDGMENT

A wise man is mightier than a strong man,
and a man of knowledge than he who has strength.

PROVERBS 24:5 RSV

FROM THE FATHER'S HEART

My child, all of the bodybuilding exercises you choose will
not add one measure to your inner character. That's not
where your strength will lie. Let Me develop in you good
judgment, a quality that comes when you seek to follow My
ways. You can win more battles with good sense than with
heavy weapons. Those who come against you cannot deny
the power within you when you let My wisdom be mightier
than the sword.

FROM A SEEKING HEART

Lord, I've tried—and failed—to talk my way out of foolish
arguments, and I've tried unsuccessfully to bluff my way out
of trouble with brute strength. I need Your good judgment—
to know what to say and when to say it; to know when to act
and when to refrain; to know when to run and when to fight.
I receive Your gift with eagerness, and I pledge to pore over
Your Word that I might discern Your will in every situation.

SIMPLE TRUTH

Cool does not mean fool.

DEMONSTRATIVENESS

"By this all men will know that you are my disciples,
if you love one another."

JOHN 13:35

FROM THE FATHER'S HEART

My child, people are not looking for a shallow hug or the kiss of betrayal. They are searching for the real thing. As a Christian, you can unashamedly show your feelings and express love to others openly. Through your demonstrativeness and My unselfish love displayed through you, you will be a testimony to others that your faith is genuine. Don't withhold affection as some do. Give love away wisely but lavishly.

FROM A SEEKING HEART

Lord, how will others know You if they see Your children unable to resolve their differences? Convict us of our selfishness, and renew our hearts again. Lord, when I think of the price You paid for me and the love You gave so freely, I recognize again the importance of loving my brothers and sisters in Christ. A family that truly loves You will spare no expense at outdoing one another in love. I choose demonstrativeness, Lord. Love through me today.

SIMPLE TRUTH

If you cannot love others here, what will you do in heaven?

PERCEPTION

*"As for what was sown on good soil,
this is he who hears the word
and understands it; he indeed bears fruit."*

MATTHEW 13:23 RSV

FROM THE FATHER'S HEART

My child, many will hear My words, but they will allow thorns—the cares of this world—to choke them out and silence My voice. Others possess such shallow faith that the roots of My Word have no place to grow. Don't let others snatch away the treasures I offer you. As you keep your ears tuned to My Word and obey what you hear Me say, I will give you perception—the ability to translate principle into action.

FROM A SEEKING HEART

Father, Your Word is like precious manna falling on my life, filling my soul and satisfying my needs. I will guard this treasure by planting its roots deep within the soil of my heart. I choose perception, Lord—to listen and look and obey what You tell me. I do not want fruitlessness to characterize my life. Let me be a fruit-bearing Christian for You!

SIMPLE TRUTH

For a seed to grow, it must have good, healthy soil.

EQUITY

*"Speak up for those who cannot speak for themselves. . . .
Speak up and judge fairly."*

PROVERBS 31:8–9

FROM THE FATHER'S HEART

My child, keep your eyes open to the injustices in My world. Speak up for the weak, the aged, the poor, the orphan, and the mistreated—all those who need someone to care. Let Me build equity in you so you can see life from all perspectives—especially from My viewpoint. You may not always please others in your decisions, but if you use My wisdom, the results will be just and fair.

FROM A SEEKING HEART

Father, my heart breaks each time I see an abandoned child or confused victim of abuse. What can I do? I am only one. I do choose to cooperate with You as You develop a sense of equity and wisdom in me. Help me see people through Your eyes, Lord. Even in small matters, I will exercise cautiousness in being fair and just. Like the little boy throwing starfish back into the ocean one by one, Lord, I can make a difference with Your help, one by one.

SIMPLE TRUTH
Follow His voice—it's the positive choice.

MORALITY

Above all else, guard your heart, for it is the wellspring of life.

PROVERBS 4:23

FROM THE FATHER'S HEART

My child, I am concerned about right and wrong in the world. And I have given My children the opportunity to make a stand and honor Me and the things Christianity represents. I will develop a strong sense of morality in you as you watch carefully the things that enter your heart and mind, so that your actions will line up with your beliefs. No one wants to listen to—or believe—hot air or hypocritical believers. Make My words your own, and live by the convictions that I dictate in My Word.

FROM A SEEKING HEART

Father, You have taught us right from wrong through parents, friends, teachers, and Your Word. In fact, no one needed to teach us how to do wrong—it comes so naturally. Lord, I pray that believing right and doing right will become my first response each time I am confronted with compromise or injustice. I choose to exercise morality by allowing the Holy Spirit to set up a watch post in my heart—and to make Your Word my first and last word.

SIMPLE TRUTH
The right thing to do is to do the right thing.

Day 306

TRANQUILITY

A tranquil mind gives life to the flesh.

PROVERBS 14:30 RSV

FROM THE FATHER'S HEART

My child, I love to quiet your soul, and it gives Me great pleasure when you come away and enjoy My presence alone, without distractions. In those moments I can turn the searchlight on your heart and show you the source of restlessness and powerlessness. I will give you tranquility, a heart at peace with Me. Then no matter what is happening around you, you can rest in Me. When I am in control of your life, the cares of this world hush—and you cease striving to know all the answers.

FROM A SEEKING HEART

Lord, everywhere You walked on earth, You cast a shadow of tranquility over those who truly came to know You. And in every heart where You live today, You are at work sweeping out the clutter, making room for peace and joy to reign. I choose this spirit of tranquility because I want my heart to be solidly under Your control. Like a child silenced by awesome wonder, I will be quiet before You, Lord. You are my peace.

SIMPLE TRUTH

The moment we cease loving God alone, tranquility will flee.

INVENTIVENESS

"Write the vision. . .so he may run who reads it.
For still the vision awaits its time."

HABAKKUK 2:2–3 RSV

FROM THE FATHER'S HEART

My child, I have planted deep treasures within My Word for those who want to find them. I long to show Myself to those who passionately pursue Me. I will give you inventiveness and reveal new truth to you as you discover and search out that truth in My Word. When I speak to you through the pages of Scripture, you can record it and act upon that truth in My perfect timing.

FROM A SEEKING HEART

Lord, I know that all truth comes from You because You are the Truth. I never want to *invent* words or messages—only to use inventiveness, creativity, and diligence in seeking to understand the truths already revealed in Your Word. Thank You for personalizing Scripture for us. Your Spirit literally highlights our needs for the day as we submit our wills to You. Lord, may my life be an eternal treasure hunt to know Your heart!

SIMPLE TRUTH

God will only reveal as much truth as we let Him.

COURTESY

*"So in everything,
do to others what you would have them do to you."*

MATTHEW 7:12

FROM THE FATHER'S HEART

My child, does simple courtesy matter? Of course it does. If My children are to make a difference in this world, they must act differently than the majority. Treating other people the way you want to be treated is practical Christianity—and it's a powerful influence to others. Some will actually judge the reality and sincerity of your beliefs by how you flesh out those beliefs in kind actions. I'll produce the fruit through you. Remember, it's the little things that count!

FROM A SEEKING HEART

Lord, I've met rude clerks and sour merchants, from grocery stores to tax offices. And I've worn my share of frowns, grumbling impatiently through checkout lines. No one likes complainers or those who live only for themselves. A friendly smile and a kind word cost nothing, but what a difference a little courtesy or a second-mile gesture can make. Lord, I will be Your representative today, dispensing free smiles and intentional kindness in the name of Jesus.

SIMPLE TRUTH

Do unto others as you would like God to do unto you.

EFFERVESCENCE

*"Whoever believes in me, as the Scripture has said,
streams of living water will flow from within him."*

JOHN 7:38

FROM THE FATHER'S HEART

My child, I love it when you get excited about Me and about something new you've discovered in My Word. And it thrills Me to see you living out My truths by faith as you help others. I know then that you are developing effervescence and are living out of the overflow of My Spirit within you. When My Spirit energizes you, others will see that supernatural glow in your life and be drawn to Me.

FROM A SEEKING HEART

Lord, I want to draw so close to You that I will be like Moses and Stephen, and others will see the glow of Jesus in my life. The more I read, the more I want to know about You. The more I know, the more I want to obey. Lord, let the effervescent glow of Your Spirit constantly flow through me. So many need to know You—and there's so little time!

SIMPLE TRUTH

Don't be a "carbonated" Christian. True effervescence bubbles, but it never goes flat.

AWARENESS

"Lord, let our eyes be opened."

MATTHEW 20:33 RSV

FROM THE FATHER'S HEART

My child, do you want to see—really see—what I am up to? Although My ways are not your ways and your comprehension will be limited, let Me open your blind eyes to the truth of My Word and give you awareness. Your part is to shut out harmful influences that steal your eyes and heart away from Me. As I make you aware of My presence and of the needs in My world, you can move in My strength to touch others.

FROM A SEEKING HEART

Lord, sometimes I see people like trees walking—because my vision is clouded by faulty judgment and poor focus. But when You clear away the cobwebs, You give me a new awareness of where You are at work. Your work becomes my work because I choose to make Your priorities mine. Who wants to live in the dark? Lord, give me heavenly twenty-twenty vision!

SIMPLE TRUTH
Take care to be aware.

INTROSPECTION

Test me, O LORD, and try me, examine my heart and my mind.

PSALM 26:2

FROM THE FATHER'S HEART

My child, there is much more I want to do for you and much more fruit I want to produce through you. Let a healthy introspection become a daily ritual. Invite Me often to turn My spotlight on your heart. Then let Me change, re-arrange, or empty the contents of your heart so that you can become a more usable vessel for Me. The process may bring pain, but the gain is worth it all.

FROM A SEEKING HEART

Lord, what a humbling, joyful experience to be used in Your service! But what a tragedy to stop short of Your dreams for my life. Lord, without engaging in morbid self-absorption or self-condemnation, I invite You once again to be the Master Designer and dream maker of my heart. Come and redecorate, rebuild, or expand this heart. Do whatever it takes to make me more like You, Lord. I choose introspec-tion—Your heavenly inspection—daily.

SIMPLE TRUTH

> *When the Master Designer finishes, we may not recognize the house, but the end product will be absolutely beautiful.*

BENEVOLENCE

*Owe no one anything, except to love one another;
for he who loves his neighbor has fulfilled the law.*

ROMANS 13:8 RSV

FROM THE FATHER'S HEART

My child, if you want to excel in something, try outdoing others in the love you show. Use My gift of benevolence to actively seek out others to love and care for, regardless of who they are. Friends will expect it, but go beyond your circle of influence. Giving yourself away through good deeds will enlarge your own joy—and the joy of the ones you help. By doing good to others, you will be following My example in love.

FROM A SEEKING HEART

Lord, You are truly my example for benevolence. Those searching for You found You in the most unlikely places: a tax collector's office, on a hillside teaching, leading a group of rough fishermen, healing a leper, or encouraging a widow. The good, the bad, and the ugly all flocked to feast on the crumbs of Your goodness—and You gave them full meals of love, dignity, and grace. Lord, I choose a benevolent attitude. Where can I show Your love today?

SIMPLE TRUTH

*Caring means sharing—of all that we are and all
that we have.*

IDEALISM

God saw all that he had made, and it was very good.

GENESIS 1:31

FROM THE FATHER'S HEART

My child, others look at My world and see total chaos. And things will deteriorate until I come back again. But you can still see the good and the beauty in life as I intended it to be by developing a sense of idealism. You can choose to preserve My standards and My beauty by being a good steward of all that I have given and done for you and by making My ways known to those who can influence My world.

FROM A SEEKING HEART

Lord, who cannot see the terror, pain, and disaster that litters a hate-filled world? But I choose to see beyond that, Lord, to a beauty that still exists: the love of family and friends, the joy of personal relationships, the grandeur of Your marvelous creation, and a purpose only You give. You created everything for us to enjoy. I will do my part to promote beauty and idealism. I will share the beauty of Christ with all who will listen.

SIMPLE TRUTH

If we cannot see beauty, we cannot see God.

COMPETENCE

*We have confidence in the Lord that you are doing
and will continue to do the things we command.*

2 THESSALONIANS 3:4

FROM THE FATHER'S HEART

My child, slothful work and idle chatter do not attract anyone to My kingdom. I have given you competence so you can do a job well. Using knowledge and skills I chose for you, your work can make a difference for Me. Always choose excellence as your standard, and choose joy as your attitude so that your work will honor Me.

FROM A SEEKING HEART

Father, thank You for giving me a part in Your kingdom's work. Although I may not feel adequate or skilled, You give me competence to accomplish any assignment. You don't ask me to compete—only to complete the work and to do it well. In so doing, Lord, I pray others will be encouraged and Your body here on earth will be strengthened.

SIMPLE TRUTH

What God begins, let no one destroy.

NARROWNESS

"Enter through the narrow gate. . . .
Small is the gate and narrow the road that leads to life,
and only a few find it."

MATTHEW 7:13–14

FROM THE FATHER'S HEART

My child, there is only one true way to life, and that is
through My Son, Jesus. Make narrowness—choosing the
road of life rather than death—an example for others. It is
following My road map as I have outlined it for your life.
That road may include difficulty, but you can be confident
that I will never lead you astray.

FROM A SEEKING HEART

Father, the world says life's answers are found through a
broad highway, but none of society's promises prove true.
That road only results in destruction and death. Lord, You
are the Way—and I choose to follow You, no matter how
many twists and turns You take me through. Not one of Your
promises has ever failed. I trust You to lead me through the
narrow way.

SIMPLE TRUTH

Entering through the narrow way usually requires
leaving behind unnecessary baggage.

COMMITMENT

Fight the good fight of faith. Take hold of the eternal life to which you were called when you made your good confession in the presence of many witnesses.

1 TIMOTHY 6:12

FROM THE FATHER'S HEART

My child, you will understand something about commitment when you let Me have your life completely for My use. Others will abandon their faith and their promises, but I want you to be different. Commitment requires a stick-to-itiveness and much sacrifice. I will help you, but you must choose to follow Me no matter what the cost. Remain loyal to Me for the rest of your life.

FROM A SEEKING HEART

Lord, I'll never forget the day I said yes to You. Truthfulness has always characterized You, but I have not always kept my intentions. I choose a new commitment today, one that says, "Jesus, I am following You." And in the presence of other accountability witnesses, I will keep my faith active and my commitment true to You—until death carries me home to You.

SIMPLE TRUTH

   Saying "I do" to Jesus means " 'til death brings us together face-to-face."

MAGNETISM

*They were not able to resist the wisdom and the spirit
by which he spake.*

ACTS 6:10 KJV

FROM THE FATHER'S HEART

My child, let Me develop magnetism in you—the reflection
of My Spirit within you that draws others to Me. It is not a
magnetic personality but a clean heart that reflects Me best.
Just like My servant Stephen, when you look into My face
and let My power operate in your life, I will be glorified in
the things you say and do.

FROM A SEEKING HEART

Lord, when Your followers looked into Your life and into
Your eyes, they could easily see a reflection of Your heavenly
Father. Your mirror never tarnished. Lord, I choose that
magnetism—to gaze constantly into Your face and in Your
Word until I begin to look like You! I long to attract others
not to me but to You, Lord!

SIMPLE TRUTH

*If others are not attracted to the Jesus in us, perhaps
our mirrors need cleaning.*

INFLUENCE

*Be careful, however, that the exercise of your freedom
does not become a stumbling block to the weak.*

1 CORINTHIANS 8:9

FROM THE FATHER'S HEART

My child, I have freely given you all things to enjoy, and you are not bound by endless laws and regulations to put and keep yourself in right standing with Me. However, your actions and words have an impact on the lives of others. Choose carefully where you invest your time, money, and energy so that others will not stumble because of you and so that Christ will be honored in everything.

FROM A SEEKING HEART

Lord, although freedom is my inheritance, it is not my license to live selfishly and foolishly. Your Word offers wise boundaries, and I choose to accept those, not only for my own good but also so that others will not stumble because of me. I choose to let my influence make a positive impact on others. I love You too much to participate in something that might be harmless to me but potentially damaging to someone else's spirit.

SIMPLE TRUTH

No matter where we go, someone is usually following.

IRIDESCENCE

The light of the righteous shines brightly.

PROVERBS 13:9

FROM THE FATHER'S HEART

My child, I love to give you iridescence so you can shine brightly for Me like a diamond. When you reflect Christ-likeness on all sides—physically, emotionally, and spiritually, others will notice and glorify Me. Maintain an intimate relationship with Me at all times. As you allow Me to chip away imperfections and polish the rough edges, you will be a radiant picture of My love to all you meet.

FROM A SEEKING HEART

Lord, how You shine—brighter than the brightest star in the heavens! Take the dullness of my heart and the scattered pieces of my life, and put together an iridescent creation that will glorify You. Even though Your jeweler's tool may hurt me, I choose to lie still in Your hands so You can shape me into something beautiful for You. Let me shine for You, Lord! I'm trading in my flaws for Your perfection.

SIMPLE TRUTH

God loves to work with diamonds in the rough.

HONOR

He shall be a vessel unto honour, sanctified,
and meet for the master's use,
and prepared unto every good work.

2 TIMOTHY 2:21 KJV

FROM THE FATHER'S HEART

My child, whether I make you a priceless vase or a crude pitcher is not your concern. I choose the purposes for all of My children. What matters is that you become a person of honor. Love Me and trust Me with all of your heart. Yield your life to Me as a clean, pure vessel, and live your life honestly and with integrity. Then you will be prepared and useful for My work at any moment.

FROM A SEEKING HEART

Father, if You can use this broken, earthly vessel of a life, You can use anyone. I have discarded all my preconceived ideas about my purpose here on earth and willingly submit to You, choosing to be a person of honor and integrity. Even little things matter, Lord, so remind me often with the nudge of Your Spirit that I belong to You—and am a "vessel of honor."

SIMPLE TRUTH

God even chooses to use cracked pots for His glory.

KNOWLEDGE

*By wisdom a house is built, and through understanding it is
established; through knowledge its rooms are filled with
rare and beautiful treasures.*

PROVERBS 24:3–4

FROM THE FATHER'S HEART

My child, a crumbling foundation, broken windows, and di-
lapidated walls are not the qualities of a solidly built house.
As you seek Me with your whole heart, I will give you
knowledge—a clear understanding of My truth. When you
follow My blueprint, your life will be like a home built on
solid ground, filled with the rare treasures of joy and purposeful living.

FROM A SEEKING HEART

Father, foolish choices bring foolish results. I choose to
wisely use the knowledge that You have given me to build
up the body of Christ and to add fragrance to the name of
Christ wherever it is proclaimed. I know the beginning of
knowledge is the fear and reverence of You. Teach me Your
truths, Lord.

SIMPLE TRUTH

It's not how much we know but how much we know
Him *that matters.*

RESPONSIBILITY

"To one he gave five talents of money, to another two talents, and to another one talent, each according to his ability."

MATTHEW 25:15

FROM THE FATHER'S HEART

My child, I love to give you responsibility so you can take seriously My assignments and handle them well. Every assigned task that you accomplish for Me shows Me I can trust you with even more. I will multiply your gifts as you use wise stewardship of your time and money and bring Me glory with those investments. There's no need to fear. I'll give you the wisdom you need to succeed!

FROM A SEEKING HEART

Lord, nothing pleases me more than hearing Your voice say, "Well done, faithful servant." At times, responsibility feels like a sack of bricks, weighing me down—like saying yes to things You never intended or shrinking from opportunities when I feel inadequate. But today, Lord, I choose to value responsibility and invest my energies—and Your gifts—to further Your kingdom's work. What an honor to serve You well!

SIMPLE TRUTH

When God calls, we can respond—with His ability!

CANDOR

He who speaks the truth gives honest evidence.

PROVERBS 12:17 RSV

FROM THE FATHER'S HEART

My child, you have no reason to fear anymore what will happen when you speak the truth. I will give you candor so you will have freedom from needing the approval of others and the ability to speak the truth frankly without partiality. When presented with an opportunity to witness for Christ or to speak up for the right, you can do so, knowing that I will give you the words to say.

FROM A SEEKING HEART

Lord, You spoke with total candor and freedom every time You ministered. People had no need to question where You stood, for You clearly stated Your purpose to honor Your Father. Lord, I choose to speak truth, whether on or off the witness stand—even if it means that others turn away. I will not compromise integrity for promotion or honesty for approval.

SIMPLE TRUTH
Wherever you go, take God with you.

INDEPENDENCE

If I were still trying to please men,
I would not be a servant of Christ.

GALATIANS 1:10

FROM THE FATHER'S HEART

My child, while I want you to be dependent on Me for all your needs, I will help you develop independence in Me also: the willingness to stand alone for Me and the desire to live for Me above all others. By declaring your independence from the world's standards and philosophies, you are choosing dependence on Me.

FROM A SEEKING HEART

Father, to love You with all my heart, soul, and mind is my desire. I choose to live in such a way that puts Your name in neon lights, not mine. Other interests call my name, but I choose to make my home wherever You are, Lord. I will exercise independence, trusting You to remove all distractions—as I live and stand alone for You.

SIMPLE TRUTH

The one who lives for Christ alone is never truly alone.

DISTINCTNESS

"You did not choose me, but I chose you and appointed you."

JOHN 15:16

FROM THE FATHER'S HEART

My child, if I lined up all my creations side by side, you would not find another exactly like you. Let Me develop distinctness in you—the recognition that you have been chosen by Me, like all of My children, for a particular purpose. Reaffirm your uniqueness in Christ, and through obedience, set your heart to accomplish that purpose.

FROM A SEEKING HEART

Father, to think that You chose me for a particular purpose—to honor You with my life—gives me great joy. Whether raising children or raising buildings, whether writing tickets or writing books, I choose to accept Your distinctness and pour my energies into loving and serving You. I will not argue with Your blueprints for my life; instead, I gratefully acknowledge whose I am. I rejoice that I belong to You, Lord!

SIMPLE TRUTH

What I do is not as important as whose I am.

CONSIDERATION

But the wisdom that comes from heaven is first of all pure;
then peace-loving, considerate, submissive,
full of mercy and good fruit.

JAMES 3:17

FROM THE FATHER'S HEART

My child, I love to see consideration in you—when you show kindness and goodwill to others because of My goodness to you. I love you and consider you My child when you place your faith in Me and accept what I did for you personally. Therefore, you can treat others with the same love and respect as special creations of Mine. Some may even choose to believe in Me because of the consideration you show as My representative.

FROM A SEEKING HEART

Lord, I could not begin to count the ways You've shown consideration to me—or to all Your children. You loved me on "dog days," feeding me not with scraps of grace but with generous portions of kindness. In the same way, Lord, I choose to open my heart and home to those who need the same consideration.

SIMPLE TRUTH

It only takes a second to give someone another chance.

EFFICIENCY

Be very careful, then, how you live—not as unwise but as wise, making the most of every opportunity, because the days are evil.

EPHESIANS 5:15–16

FROM THE FATHER'S HEART

My child, if I revealed everything about the future to you, you could neither stand it nor would you understand it. None of My children knows how long they will live. I will develop efficiency in you when you take care to do a job well and when you make the best use of your time and energy. Your purpose is not to cross off lists, however. In all you do, choose the pursuits in life that count—those that make a difference in My kingdom.

FROM A SEEKING HEART

Father, life is too short to live any other way but wisely. Thank You for forgiving wasted moments and destructive habits of the past. Like a patient who has been declared free of a previously labeled "terminal illness," I choose to spend my days in work that honors You. I will block out distractions that hinder effectiveness—and apply all my energies into kingdom work.

SIMPLE TRUTH

Our former loves are in the past—only what's done for Christ will last.

INNOVATIVENESS

"The God of heaven will give us success.
We his servants will start rebuilding."

NEHEMIAH 2:20

FROM THE FATHER'S HEART

My child, don't get too comfortable. Are you willing to move beyond your comfort zone? I will use you as a catalyst for change. As you obey the promptings of My Spirit to do something new or to bring about a needed change for growth, you will learn the quality of innovativeness. Find out where I'm working, and join Me. Let Me use you wherever I want to accomplish My work.

FROM A SEEKING HEART

Father, shake us and remake us if necessary to keep us from standing still and growing stagnant. No matter how old or young we are, You can still teach us new ways of doing things. Change must occur if growth will come. I am willing to learn innovativeness and to "set my heart on pilgrimage"—moving when You say, "Move," content if You whisper, "Stay."

SIMPLE TRUTH

A rut can be a grave or a cradle. Either way, if we
don't get out of it, we will never grow.

COHERENCE

From him the whole body,
joined and held together by every supporting ligament,
grows and builds itself up in love, as each part does its work.

EPHESIANS 4:16

FROM THE FATHER'S HEART

My child, when My "family" sticks together, there is strength in numbers. I will give you coherence so you can think, move, and act in harmony with yourself and others for a common goal. I need every person to listen to My voice and follow in obedience. As a member of My body on earth, you can work together with others to make My ways and will known.

FROM A SEEKING HEART

Father, whether I am a foot, a hand, an eye, or a mouth, I will use what I have wisely to build up the body of Christ. Keep my "parts" oiled and energized with Your Spirit, Lord, so I will harmonize with the rest of Your children. Together we can act coherently to love each other. What a joy to see Your body on earth grow in grace and wisdom—and to reach out to grow new disciples!

SIMPLE TRUTH

The family that does not "stick" together will most
likely be sick together.

THANKFULNESS

Give thanks to the LORD, call on his name;
make known among the nations what he has done.

PSALM 105:1

FROM THE FATHER'S HEART

My child, there is nothing more attractive than a thankful, contented heart. I love to see thankfulness in you—that attitude of gratitude that wells up inside you in response to My goodness. It means living each day in praise and thanksgiving to Me and giving Me credit for every good and perfect gift in your life. A grateful heart means you are submitted to My will—and that makes Me want to bless you even more.

FROM A SEEKING HEART

Father, how can I say thanks? A thousand times a day my heart cries out in thankfulness to You—for blessings undeserved, for grace unreserved; for forgiveness, health, shelter, food; for lessons learned; for everything good; for family, friends; for a purpose-filled life—too many things to count! Lord, today I will utter no complaint. All day long I will boast of You—and give thanks!

SIMPLE TRUTH

Gratitude attracts; complaining repels.

OPEN-MINDEDNESS

*Let the wise listen and add to their learning,
and let the discerning get guidance.*

PROVERBS 1:5

FROM THE FATHER'S HEART

My child, only fools blurt out all they think they know. Let
Me develop in you a spirit of open-mindedness—a willingness to listen to all sides of a question before making a decision. Remember before you speak to weigh every matter
in the light of My wisdom. Then you will be better prepared
to give a fair and honest reply.

FROM A SEEKING HEART

Lord, when You talked with people, You often asked them
questions and always allowed them a hearing before responding. Many times You even refrained from speaking
when wisdom demanded silence. I choose to be open-
minded like You, Lord, to allow people an opportunity to
express their thoughts and feelings. I can learn from others
by listening and not rushing to wrong conclusions. I will
trust You for correct and wise answers that honor You.

SIMPLE TRUTH

*A closed mind is like a sealed cave where nothing can
grow.*

MILDNESS

*Be completely humble and gentle; be patient,
bearing with one another in love.*

Ephesians 4:2

From the Father's Heart

My child, responding in anger only drives people away. Instead, let your words be choice morsels of grace that heap coals of shame on those who goad you. When you act with mildness instead of reacting in anger, I can use your words to bring harmony and peace to others. Mildness will help you listen patiently to others and refuse to wear unbecoming feelings on your shoulders.

From a Seeking Heart

Lord, no wonder You were called the Lamb of God. You treated others with mildness and gentleness, and even in the midst of chaos, Your Spirit was in perfect peace. I choose mildness, not anger, especially when dealing with "irregular" people. You have been superpatient with me, always listening to my cries and petitions. I refuse grudges and will not be easily offended. We all make mistakes—especially me!

Simple Truth

Listening opens the door to another's heart.

FAITHFULNESS

A faithful man will abound with blessings.

PROVERBS 28:20 RSV

FROM THE FATHER'S HEART

My child, I do not require that you observe a set of rules to gain My approval. It is not your performance that I judge but your acceptance of My salvation—the gift of My Son as payment for what you could never do. It is a relationship that I desire. However, I desire and expect your faithfulness because of your devotion to Me. Faithfulness means giving Me 100 percent of your time and energy and choosing to serve Me diligently because of My love for you. That's the least you can do. I take pleasure in blessing faithfulness.

FROM A SEEKING HEART

Father, if there is one thing I have learned in my life, it is that You are faithful! You always keep Your Word! How I long to be known as a faithful follower of Yours! I choose to love You, to serve You, to follow Your commands, and to listen closely for Your voice daily. Lord, with Your help, I choose faithfulness as a way of life!

SIMPLE TRUTH

All great relationships are built on truth and faithfulness.

FLEXIBILITY

Restore to me the joy of thy salvation,
and uphold me with a willing spirit.

PSALM 51:12 RSV

FROM THE FATHER'S HEART

My child, your ideas and plans are based upon earthly knowledge. Keep flexibility as a guide for the future. You have no idea how I may change events—and people—to fit into My plans and My purpose because My thoughts are heavenly. Flexibility will come when you are willing to let Me rearrange your life to suit My purpose. It is fitting in with My plans without complaining or demanding your own way.

FROM A SEEKING HEART

Lord, instead of bending out of shape when changes occur at the last minute, when someone thwarts my plans, or if another challenges my ideas, I will train myself to look behind the reason. I will be open to alternatives and flexibility for change, realizing that You are the blessed controller of all things. And in the words of one character who realized the importance of flexibility, I will agree: "There is a God—and I'm not Him." You are in control, Lord!

SIMPLE TRUTH

Wise believers never set their plans in concrete.

GLADNESS

Thou hast put gladness in my heart.

Psalm 4:7 kjv

From the Father's Heart

My child, take time to observe some fragrant lilies or the chirping sparrows. Do they fret about where to find the next worm or how vibrant their colors will look in spring? Neither should you. Accept gladness as a gift I give you when you abandon your cares and thoughts to Me. As you focus your eyes away from yourself, I will put a spirit of cheerfulness in your heart that will help brighten the lives of others—and bring you peace.

From a Seeking Heart

Father, when You placed Your Spirit within me, You filled me with Yourself. Forgive me for not appropriating gladness, which characterizes itself in the gift of joy and contentment. Life is not about me; it's all about loving You—and loving others. Transform my idle thoughts and cares into the cheerful spirit You intended—so I can be a light that turns others toward You.

Simple Truth
Let our laughter be long—let our anger be short.

GRACEFULNESS

Pleasant words are a honeycomb,
sweet to the soul and healing to the bones.

PROVERBS 16:24

FROM THE FATHER'S HEART

My child, My message is not a hammer with which to pound truth into others; nor is it a plunger to flush out unwanted pests. Let Me develop gracefulness in your life so you can speak and act wisely in a way that attracts, not repels, others to Me. As I give you opportunities, share honestly, gently, and lovingly about the things God has done for you. My Word is a sword in itself and will cut to the truth— if you will let Me do the work.

FROM A SEEKING HEART

Lord, I cannot force myself into someone's life; I must gain a hearing as You open the door. Let me do so with the graceful strength of a ballet dancer who has been disciplined to move with the music. You are the music, Lord, and I will be Your "dancer" as I use gracefulness—with strong conviction—to turn ordinary moments into supernatural healing opportunities for You.

SIMPLE TRUTH

The sweet gift of salvation is built on love, not fear.

INTENSITY

*Dear children, let us not love with words or tongue
but with actions and in truth.*

1 JOHN 3:18

FROM THE FATHER'S HEART

My child, intensity does not mean a propensity for introspection. The kind of intensity I want for you is intentionally treating My commands with seriousness. It is not giving
flippant lip service but loving, serving, and giving with your
whole being as you are tuned to My Spirit. Who will believe
you if you say one thing but do another?

FROM A SEEKING HEART

Lord, so many of Your disciples in Scripture followed You
with intensity. Yet it was not until Your Spirit engulfed
them after Your resurrection that they truly believed the
power of Your words. Lord, let my words be Your words
speaking through me. And when I say I love others, I
choose to prove that love by following through with intense
obedience and sacrifice. That's what You did for me.

SIMPLE TRUTH

Good sense chooses to be intense about love and obedience.

MINDFULNESS

*Who can proclaim the mighty acts of the LORD
or fully declare his praise?*

PSALM 106:2

FROM THE FATHER'S HEART

My child, as long as My world exists, there will always come fall, winter, spring, and summer, the moon and the stars, and the sun to shine upon you. My beauty is a treasure to those who seek—and look with their hearts. Always keep mindfulness in your life—an acute awareness of Me and of My creation. I love for you to worship and praise Me as a personal God and living Savior as you enjoy the world I have given you.

FROM A SEEKING HEART

Lord, when I look into the face of the moon or bask in the spell of a perfect day; when I stand in the presence of a towering cliff, listen to the rippling of a crystal clear stream, or hear the sweet strains of a newborn's cry, I am mindful of Your awesome character. Praise wells up and overflows like a gushing fountain as my heart cries out, "Yes, Lord! Yes!"

SIMPLE TRUTH

Beautiful places can always be found by the heart that searches diligently.

LIGHTHEARTEDNESS

Be joyful always.

1 THESSALONIANS 5:16

FROM THE FATHER'S HEART

My child, are you tempted to pull back and enter a shell of seriousness each time hard challenges come your way? Remember to let lightheartedness help you take one day at a time with a heart full of trust. Delight each day in bringing joy and humor into the lives of others—refusing to "sweat the small stuff."

FROM A SEEKING HEART

Father, difficulties come to us all. I can choose to withdraw or let them bounce off my outer shell of lightheartedness. When I choose to laugh at myself—and shake off accompanying worries—I can live peacefully and joyfully, knowing You are in charge of everything. Because joy is contagious, my lighthearted attitude may even help to lighten the loads of others.

SIMPLE TRUTH

Laughter mends the body and sweetens the soul.

VITALITY

Our sufficiency is of God; who also hath made us able ministers of the new testament; not of the letter, but of the spirit.

2 CORINTHIANS 3:5–6 KJV

FROM THE FATHER'S HEART

My child, I want you to be a life-giver, not a spirit-killer. I will develop vitality in you—the freedom from legalistic rules and inhibitions. Vitality is the supernatural grace and strength that comes when you ask Me to fill you with My Holy Spirit and accept My cleansing work. People need life—and you can tell them where and how to find it.

FROM A SEEKING HEART

Lord, our efforts to clean ourselves up or make us worthy in Your sight will all fail. You did that for us when You died for us and rose again. I will be Your messenger of vitality, declaring that supernatural freedom we have and can find in You. You came to fulfill the Law, Lord, and to free us from unnecessary bondage. I choose that vitality for myself so I will not be labeled a "grace-killer" but a fresh breath of life-giving love for You, Jesus!

SIMPLE TRUTH

Grace is the place we go when life has dealt a heavy blow, and grace will lead us home again, where life really begins.

APPROACHABILITY

Surely you desire truth in the inner parts;
you teach me wisdom in the inmost place.

PSALM 51:6

FROM THE FATHER'S HEART

My child, hiding out is for those whose hearts have been darkened by fear or mistrust. Dark corners grow stale and musty without the Light. Let Me give you approachability so you can allow others a glimpse of your life close-up. Approachability is choosing not to distance yourself from Me or others but to open your heart and become vulnerable to My wishes. I will show you the truth so you can be free indeed.

FROM A SEEKING HEART

Lord, You made Yourself available—and approachable—to a band of disciples as You lived with them and taught them daily for three years. You held nothing back except what they could not understand at the time. Your life was an open door where others could enter and find comfort, rest, strength, and healing. Lord, I, too, choose approachability so others can see the real You. Hiding behind walls of indifference or fear helps no one. Lord, the welcome mat is out and the door is open—to You and to others.

SIMPLE TRUTH

If we spend our lives hiding the Truth, who will find it?

VALUE

For God so loved the world, that he gave his only begotten Son, that whosoever believeth in him should not perish, but have everlasting life.

John 3:16 KJV

From the Father's Heart

My child, how much do you think you are worth? How you live, how you think, how you respond to Me and others reveals the answer to that question. You are of great value to Me because of the price I placed on your life when I gave My Son to die in your place. You are indeed My special treasure. It pleases Me when you respond to My love by giving Me your life in service—but your value does not depend on anything you do. It's who you *are* to Me that makes you valuable.

From a Seeking Heart

Lord, we often let crude barbs from thoughtless critics define our worth instead of accepting our value in You. Thank You for the reminder of how much You prize me as Your child—and that I am of great worth to You. You proved that by sending Your Son to tell us so in person! I choose to believe You, Lord, and I will act as a child of great value—a child of the King.

Simple Truth

There is no way to measure the value of one soul to Christ.

RELIABILITY

*Moreover it is required of stewards that they
be found trustworthy.*

1 CORINTHIANS 4:2 RSV

FROM THE FATHER'S HEART

My child, I have given you unique tools, for which you are
accountable to Me. When you can handle these faithfully, I
will develop reliability in you and trust you with even more
responsibility. I long to expand your influence and give you
more opportunities to make My name and message known.
People need Me, Child. Will you be My reliable messenger?

FROM A SEEKING HEART

Lord, I will not shy away from the responsibility of being
Your child. I will be Your servant, acting with reliability and
faithfulness. I know if I squander my opportunities, I cannot
expect You to bless me with more. And yet Your forgiveness
knows no end. With Your help, I choose to concentrate on
what will help, not hinder, my completion of those assigned
tasks. Thank You, Lord, for believing in me.

SIMPLE TRUTH
Reliability is not a liability.

PRECISION

*That which was from the beginning, which we have heard,
which we have seen with our eyes. . .this we proclaim
concerning the Word of life.*

1 JOHN 1:1

FROM THE FATHER'S HEART

My child, too many interpret My words as fables and fig-
ments of the imagination instead of absolute truth. How
will you respond when someone questions your beliefs? I
will teach you precision so you can report and live truth as I
reveal it to you through My Word. Precision chooses My
standard of excellence and accuracy as your own. Listen; believe; follow; obey. The "facts," when enveloped in My
Spirit, will speak for themselves.

FROM A SEEKING HEART

Lord, no one spoke with more precision than You. To Your
Father's life and message, You lived true. You spoke the
truth; You are the Truth. I choose to live with precision—on
target with Your precise purpose for me—and to help others find their purposes in life by accurately pointing them to
the Way and the Truth.

SIMPLE TRUTH

> *People may question our knowledge; but they cannot
> steal our testimony.*

VIRTUE

A righteous man who walks in his integrity—
blessed are his sons after him!

PROVERBS 20:7 RSV

FROM THE FATHER'S HEART

My child, your life is a living, breathing testimony of My power and grace. Some will decide whether to accept Me or not by observing your life and your faith. That's why I take such great care to develop virtue in you—the character of Christ exemplified in your life daily. As you walk honestly with Me by your side, I will develop virtue and moral integrity in your life.

FROM A SEEKING HEART

Father, in a world where morality is almost obsolete, I choose to hold on to a fading quality called virtue. I am not perfect in my actions, and I need Your power daily to stay true. But with all of my heart, I want to look like You and let virtue characterize my life. If You believe in me enough to shape a broken piece of clay into a usable vessel, I can honor You by living a life of moral integrity and purity.

SIMPLE TRUTH

A child of God is respected not for being a prude but
for being prudent.

AGELESSNESS

*"Therefore, whoever humbles himself like this child
is the greatest in the kingdom of heaven."*

MATTHEW 18:4

FROM THE FATHER'S HEART

My child, who told you that growing older made you useless?
At age eighty, Caleb drove out the enemies who possessed his
God-given land. Moses answered God's call at eighty. Let me
give you agelessness—the ability to greet each day with an ex-
pectant and humble heart. I will develop this spirit of youthfulness in you when you approach My throne—and My
Word—not as a child but with a childlike attitude.

FROM A SEEKING HEART

Father, You have promised us we will bear fruit even in old
age; yet You challenge us to live as little children. I choose
to drop all pretense and pride and dedicate myself to live
humbly before You, Lord. I will wake up each morning with
a childlike heart filled with joy and a youthful outlook, em-
bracing one desire: to make my days count for You. Lord, I
choose to live with an ageless mentality—living life wisely
as if there were no tomorrow, trusting You daily as if I had
strength forever.

SIMPLE TRUTH

A child's arms are always open to embrace God's heart.

SENTIMENTALITY

God can testify how I long for all of you
with the affection of Christ Jesus.

PHILIPPIANS 1:8

FROM THE FATHER'S HEART

My child, not a day passes without My thinking of you. I love
you so much that I have planned every day of your life carefully and purposefully. I've treasured every joy and reminisced
with your every celebration. Let Me develop a similar senti-
mentality in you so that you value people more than things. I
want to increase in you an intense longing and joy for Me,
others, and the things of My kingdom. Most of all, I want
you to love Me and others as deeply as I have loved you.

FROM A SEEKING HEART

Father, deliver me from the faulty, shallow thinking that
things can replace people. I choose a spirit of sentimental-
ity, valuing what You value—people and relationships. I will
take time to care about others and let them know how much
I love and appreciate them. Only You can put a Godlike
love in my heart that will feel that deeply about others' cares
and concerns.

SIMPLE TRUTH

Love gives the best it has to offer; then it gives even
more.

PLIABLENESS

Yet, O LORD, you are our Father. We are the clay,
you are the potter; we are all the work of your hand.

ISAIAH 64:8

FROM THE FATHER'S HEART

My child, would you rather sit idle on a shelf or serve Me as a useful vessel? If the answer is usefulness, then let Me develop pliability in you—the willingness to be molded, shaped, or broken as I see fit. If I allow persecution, illness, or injustice to shape your character, don't be alarmed. Just trust Me and rest in My hands. Allow Me to perfect My desire and purpose for your life.

FROM A SEEKING HEART

Lord, just when I think I cannot stand another moment of Your painful shaping, You rest the wheel and pat over my imperfections with a gentle, soothing hand. I choose pliableness, no matter how deep the pain, no matter how severe the breaking. Because, Lord, to fulfill Your purpose for my life—to be like You, Jesus—is my highest joy.

SIMPLE TRUTH

What God breaks, He always remakes.

SHREWDNESS

Therefore put on the full armor of God,
so that when the day of evil comes,
you may be able to stand your ground.

EPHESIANS 6:13

FROM THE FATHER'S HEART

My child, you cannot walk in heavy armor of your own devices. Like My servant David, who killed a giant armed with only a slingshot and a few smooth stones, you must shed your outdated defenses and let Me give you shrewdness. When you dress in the armor I have prepared for you, you can defend your faith and stand firm against harmful influences.

FROM A SEEKING HEART

Lord, You've told us that one can chase a thousand when You are the Captain of our plans. To walk anywhere without You, especially into enemy territory, would be both foolish and self-destructive. Lord, I choose Your shrewdness by wearing Your protective armor. As a child of God, dressed in Your clothes of righteousness, truth, faith, peace, salvation, prayer, and equipped with the Spirit, I am always prepared.

SIMPLE TRUTH

Only fools enter battle unprepared.

EXPERTISE

For this reason I remind you to fan into flame the gift of God,
which is in you through the laying on of my hands.

2 TIMOTHY 1:6

FROM THE FATHER'S HEART

My child, I've chosen carefully to match My tasks with available servants. You may feel unqualified, but I will give you expertise as you let Me develop your full potential. Empowered by the gifts I give you, you can use every opportunity to train others in this Christian walk. Keep studying, stay disciplined, and let the spark I've begun in you grow into a flaming fire of devotion for Me.

FROM A SEEKING HEART

Lord, even when I can see only the embers of a fruit-filled life, I will fan that flame—the gift of Your Spirit—so I can keep learning and growing. Give me Your expertise, Lord, for I have none of my own. An amateur at best, I will keep preparing and keep saying "Yes" to You so I can, in turn, disciple others for Your service. I know it only takes one spark to get a fire growing.

SIMPLE TRUTH
Don't prematurely end what the Holy Spirit begins.

JUBILANCE

Sing psalms and hymns and spiritual songs
with thankfulness in your hearts to God.

COLOSSIANS 3:16 RSV

FROM THE FATHER'S HEART

My child, does your spirit dance when you come into My presence? Does your heart leap for joy at the sound of My name? If so, you are learning jubilance, the expression of a free spirit in love with Me. When you are overwhelmed with My joy, you can openly and unashamedly praise Me in jubilant song. You have great reason to celebrate! I love to hear the praises of My children!

FROM A SEEKING HEART

Lord, how can I keep quiet when I think of all You've done for me? How can my faith stand still when I consider Your character? With hands lifted high and heart bowed low, I sing praise to You, Lord, with jubilance! I love You, Lord—and I'm desperate to know You and love You more and more. I will keep the song alive that You began in me—and I choose to celebrate You with great joy!

SIMPLE TRUTH

Worship is not an order of service; it is an attitude of the heart.

CORDIALITY

*Do not let any unwholesome talk come out of your mouths,
but only what is helpful for building others up according
to their needs, that it may benefit those who listen.*

EPHESIANS 4:29

FROM THE FATHER'S HEART

My child, everyone needs a little more love. Don't you? Let
Me use you to affirm others with words of love and encouragement by developing cordiality in you. You can help
strengthen the body of Christ by meeting the practical and
emotional needs of others in little ways. As you deal with
others, limit your comments to words that build up, and
avoid those that destroy another.

FROM A SEEKING HEART

Father, You have affirmed and reaffirmed Your love for me
daily. The truth of Your Word washes out every negative arrow
that pierces my mind. I choose to be a messenger of positive
affirmation, creatively strengthening others through words of
praise and encouragement. I will lift up the downhearted and
speak kindness to the discouraged. Most of all, I will tell them
how much they are loved by their heavenly Father. Lord, I
choose cordiality today. Who needs a good word today?

SIMPLE TRUTH
Be the first to run the second mile.

COORDINATION

But they gave themselves first to the Lord
and then to us in keeping with God's will.

2 CORINTHIANS 8:5

FROM THE FATHER'S HEART

My child, I will develop coordination in you so you can order
your life like a wheel. When you give Me first place, I will become the hub around which all of your activities and interests
flow. Whatever activities I sanction, place these on each
spoke. Then, as others ask for your time, weigh the requests
in light of the priorities I have given you. If the requests agree
with My priorities, accept. If not, politely refuse. Above all,
I want to be first in your life.

FROM A SEEKING HEART

Father, help me eliminate the soul-sucking activities,
thoughts, and interests that pull me in the opposite direction—even though those things might appear "good." I
choose to coordinate everything that is wholesome, profitable, and best according to Your will and to live a life with
You at the center. Order my steps, Lord. Your plans are my
plans.

SIMPLE TRUTH

If we have no margin in our lives, it is impossible to
maintain balance.

FERVOR

Never be lacking in zeal,
but keep your spiritual fervor, serving the Lord.

ROMANS 12:11

FROM THE FATHER'S HEART

My child, anyone who says working in My kingdom is dull has either never experienced My real power or is on the verge of burnout. Let Me infuse you with fervor so you can look at your work as an exciting service to Me and give it your full energy and enthusiasm. When you serve Me with fervor, I will bless you and others around you.

FROM A SEEKING HEART

Lord, whenever the lightbulb of my life was flickering, You replaced it with the full force of Your spiritual power. Every day is an exciting challenge to make a difference for You. Whether it's pushing a broom or a computer button, organizing an office or a child's room, creating a solution or a masterpiece—I can do Your special tasks with fervor and excitement knowing I am doing it for the Lord.

SIMPLE TRUTH

Once we have experienced true love, nothing else satisfies.

INTELLIGENCE

*An intelligent mind acquires knowledge,
and the ear of the wise seeks knowledge.*

PROVERBS 18:15 RSV

FROM THE FATHER'S HEART

My child, what you know may be just as important as who
you know. And when I bless you with intelligence, you can
have both. Intelligence will come when you prepare yourself
adequately with My Word and apply it daily to your life.
You can know Me—and know what I am saying through
My Word. I will be faithful to teach you, to answer your
seeking heart, and to fill you with My truth.

FROM A SEEKING HEART

Father, the more I know You, the more I realize how little
intelligence I really have according to the world's standards.
But the more I love You, the hungrier I am to understand
more so I can act wisely and follow Your commands clearly.
I choose to pursue the intelligence that You give—the life-
changing-in-your-heart kind. Teach me, Lord. I'm hungry
for You!

SIMPLE TRUTH

*When we are members of the CIA (Christ in Action),
His intelligence is enough.*

MERIT

And God raised us up with Christ and seated us with him
in the heavenly realms in Christ Jesus.

EPHESIANS 2:6

FROM THE FATHER'S HEART

My child, I have given you great merit—the undeserved honor and privilege of becoming My own child. Nothing you can do will change that place you have in My heart. Once you have chosen to be a member of the family of God, you can truly rejoice in knowing that you belong to Me. I have placed you on the top shelf of My heart! You don't feel deserving? It's not where you are or what you do—it's whose you are. You belong to Me, My child! And I placed you there so that My grace can be seen through you.

FROM A SEEKING HEART

Father, I do not deserve Your merit, but I accept this honor and choose to live in the joyful knowledge that I am a King's kid. Just to think about Your adoption of me into Your family—and all the inherent privileges that position affords—Lord, it's more than I can comprehend! One day we will all celebrate together in one final resting place of honor. In the meantime, Lord, I choose to honor You here—in everything I do!

SIMPLE TRUTH

We need to see ourselves as God sees us.

COMPREHENSION

. . .in order that they may know the mystery of God.

COLOSSIANS 2:2

FROM THE FATHER'S HEART

My child, you will not fully understand My nature and everything I do in this lifetime. But when I fill your whole being with an awareness of My presence, you can respond with a positive declaration of your partial comprehension. And as you meet with Me daily, I will be faithful to shed light on your comprehension by giving you *rhema*—a personal, enlightened word from My heart to yours.

FROM A SEEKING HEART

Lord, Your ways are past finding out, and Your thoughts are so far above mine, I could never come close to complete understanding. Yet I thank You for the comprehension—the limited knowledge You give that makes me cry out in spontaneous praise to You: "Abba! Father! Daddy! Lord! Master! Friend! King of Kings!" When I enter Your holy presence, I feel as if I have found hidden treasure. In those moments You would have to strike me with dumbness like Zechariah to arrest my speech—for I cannot keep silent.

SIMPLE TRUTH

Prayer is the posture of the heart, an attitude of praise, an understanding of the Spirit that fellowships moment by moment with the Master.

Day 358

QUALITY

*May the God of peace. . .equip you with everything good for
doing his will, and may he work in us what is pleasing to him,
through Jesus Christ, to whom be glory for ever and ever.*

HEBREWS 13:20–21

FROM THE FATHER'S HEART

My child, let all your work be done with quality—a mark of
excellence that belongs to all My children. Hasty preparation and shoddy workmanship should never characterize
your contributions. I have given you everything you need
for accomplishing My work. Remember, you are serving a
King. I want not just your best—I want you to give Me your
all because you love Me. Isn't that what I gave to you?

FROM A SEEKING HEART

Father, You have equipped me with skill, knowledge, power,
and motivation. What excuse do I have for offering less
than quality work? Everything I am and everything I own
belongs to You. Empowered by You, I choose quality and
excellence as my goal—for You deserve nothing less!

SIMPLE TRUTH

If we provide the willingness, God will do the work.

SPIRIT

*Praise the LORD, O my soul;
all my inmost being, praise his holy name.*

PSALM 103:1

FROM THE FATHER'S HEART

My child, have you ever heard of a "spirit" award? Well, I will award each of My children with spirit—a contagious and powerful energy—when you seek Me with your whole heart and soul. As you ask My Holy Spirit to fill your own, you will find praise welling up in waves—far greater than any earthly "waves" of enthusiasm at an earthly sports event. You can use that supernatural energy to make My name known everywhere you go.

FROM A SEEKING HEART

Lord, no matter what is going on around me, I will be a cheerleader for You, leading others boldly to Your throne. I will search for You and walk daily in Your presence. I choose spirit that will flow from Your own Spirit—an enthusiasm that buckets of cold water can never wash away. A thousand cheers for You, Jesus! Hallelujah to Your name!

SIMPLE TRUTH

Praise hushes in God's presence yet leaps to sing His name.

JOYFULNESS

*"My soul glorifies the Lord and my spirit rejoices
in God my Savior."*

LUKE 1:46–47

FROM THE FATHER'S HEART

My child, long before I spoke the world into being, I created a way for joyfulness to enter the earth and make its way into your heart. Because of My good gift, My own Son, Jesus, you now have a reason to rejoice and give thanks daily. Joyfulness will come when you can recognize the full meaning of that precious gift and appropriate everything He came to do in your life.

FROM A SEEKING HEART

Lord, people have long searched for true meaning, for peace, and for joy. We've hunted in all the wrong places, and our pursuits have led us to garbage dumps littered with broken dreams. But, Lord, true joyfulness is accepting the good news of Jesus—His birth, His death, His resurrection—for ourselves. It is knowing Jesus personally! I choose to treasure this gift, to share it, and to be joyful, regardless of my circumstances—because the joy You give is permanent.

SIMPLE TRUTH

*Joy is the fragrant residue of a life broken, forgiven,
and spilled out for the Master.*

GENEROSITY

Give, and it shall be given unto you;
good measure, pressed down,
and shaken together, and running over.

LUKE 6:38 KJV

FROM THE FATHER'S HEART

My child, true joy loves to give and give and give. Let Me develop in you a heart filled with generosity—giving out of a heart of love and thankfulness, regardless of your situation in life. Because I have blessed you with so much, I expect you to circulate My wealth—and the time and gifts I have given you—with others in the name of Jesus. Remember, I gave you the best gift I had. I withhold no good thing from those who walk obediently with Me.

FROM A SEEKING HEART

Lord, Your example of generosity matches none. You gave everything to me! How exciting that You create not only the provisions for our own needs, but You allow us to meet others' needs, too. Lord, I choose to share with generosity at all times throughout the year, realizing that I can never outgive You. Thank You for giving Your all for me!

SIMPLE TRUTH

The best treasures can't be bought or sold; they are gifts
from the heart—and they never grow old.

INSPIRATION

The heavens declare the glory of God;
the skies proclaim the work of his hands.

PSALM 19:1

FROM THE FATHER'S HEART

My child, I have created a story with My handiwork. Have you read it lately? Look and listen carefully, and I will fuel your inspiration—a spirit in touch with My beauty. As you savor the true beauty of My work, you can respond by inspiring others—through music, encouraging words, or deeds of kindness. Tell *My* story—with your own creative life stories. As I inspire you, others will read and listen to you and believe in Me.

FROM A SEEKING HEART

Lord, where do I start? From breathtaking sunrise to colorful sunsets, Your world spells beauty. I will take the inspiration You place in me and create a true work of my heart—unique with my gifts and Your blessing upon it. You are behind every bird's song, every leaf's rustle, every canyon's echo, every child's laughter. You created it all—for us! With Your help, I will inspire others as You have inspired me. Above all, may they see Your character and Your signature upon everything I "create" for You.

SIMPLE TRUTH

What God breathes in, we breathe out.

VALIDITY

If we live in the Spirit, let us also walk in the Spirit.

GALATIANS 5:25 KJV

FROM THE FATHER'S HEART

My child, others will often look to you for a picture of Me. What do they see right now? With My help, you can walk close to Me, not demanding perfection of yourself but seeking a relationship that will conform you to My image and give validity to the name "Christian." If you stray, run back to My arms quickly to avoid damaging your reputation and Mine. Keep our fellowship sweet. My Spirit is at work in you daily—and will always be working—to make you look like Me. Make yourself available, and I will do the rest.

FROM A SEEKING HEART

Lord, how can I measure up to the standards of a "healthy" Christian? How can I, so weak in my own strength, give a true picture of who You really are? Grace frees us from that bondage! Lord, I choose today to live a spirit-filled life—to get so close to You that You are seen in my walk, in my talk, in my face, and in my emotions. May I be a valid example of a broken life made whole and complete in You. When I look in the mirror, I long to see Your face there, not mine!

SIMPLE TRUTH
The closer He gets, the sweeter we'll be.

SAGACITY

A wise man fears the LORD and shuns evil.

PROVERBS 14:16

FROM THE FATHER'S HEART

My child, the simple and foolish run headlong into danger, like a sheep following others senselessly off a cliff. Let Me develop sagacity in you so you can sense evil motives and perceive danger. Allow My Word to protect your mind and to sharpen your instincts so that truth and wisdom are easier to discern. I know My sheep—and because you know Me, too, you can hear My voice clearly if you truly listen.

FROM A SEEKING HEART

Father, I have played the fool, and I have tried to walk where angels dare not tread. But today I am choosing to live with sagacity—purposefully letting Your Word wash over and cleanse and protect my mind from anything harmful that would try to steal my thoughts or affections. I will remain in Your Word and in Your presence until I find the answers—and the strength I need. And then, bathed in Your Spirit, I will move out confidently on the offense with You, ready to defeat my enemies.

SIMPLE TRUTH

Stay close to Jesus. The Good Shepherd will never lead us astray.

INGENUITY

All scripture is inspired by God and profitable for teaching, for reproof, for correction, and for training in righteousness.

2 TIMOTHY 3:16 RSV

FROM THE FATHER'S HEART

My child, has someone tried to convince you that your efforts are futile, that your talents are few, and that your ideas don't matter? I have given you ingenuity—a unique viewpoint with creative outlets to express yourself. You can prepare yourself through My Word to more effectively let My ways be known. If you make sure My Spirit is inspiring your words and if your desire is to honor Me, there is no limit to how I can use you.

FROM A SEEKING HEART

Father, how exciting to know the variety of ways You choose to complete Your work on earth. Although at times I may feel inferior, I choose to believe the truth of Your Word. I will use the ingenuity You gave me to express the character of Christ within me—creatively, uniquely, any way I can, Lord. I am an awesome child of Yours and will believe that daily because I belong to an awesome Father God! Together we can make a unique difference!

SIMPLE TRUTH

There is only one way to become God's child, but there are many ways to serve Him.

HEAVEN BOUND

But our citizenship is in heaven.

PHILIPPIANS 3:20

FROM THE FATHER'S HEART

My child, did you know that you are in a lifetime school of learning? My heart's desire is that you will become heaven bound—realizing that this life is only a temporary dwelling place and preparation for eternity. Setting your heart on heaven diminishes your disappointments here on earth and strengthens your hope for a better day. I have been building My character in you one day at a time—so that one day you will truly be like your Father in your real home in heaven.

FROM A SEEKING HEART

Father, I try to visualize it all—golden streets, jeweled gates, angelic chorus, bright lights, white robes. But most of all, seeing You—face-to-face. No other joy compares; no other treasure equals its value; no other thought consumes me like the anticipation of seeing You, Lord, in all Your glory. Indeed I am heaven bound, and I know that every pain, loss, injustice, and disappointment will fade when I hear those final words, "Welcome home, Child! I've been waiting for you."

SIMPLE TRUTH

If we were allowed one glimpse of heaven, we would not cling to earth—because home, after all, is where God is.

Perhaps you have never made the wonderful discovery of knowing Jesus Christ in an intimate, personal way. If He has placed such a desire in your heart, may I share with you some simple steps so you can become acquainted with Jesus and be a child of God forever?

1. Admit the sin in your life and the need in your heart for God (Romans 3:23).

2. Acknowledge that Jesus loves you and that He died for your sin (John 3:16).

3. Recognize that His salvation is a gift and not something earned (Ephesians 2:8–9; Romans 6:23).

4. Ask Jesus to forgive you, to come into your life, and to fill you with His personal, intimate presence (Revelation 3:20).

5. By faith, thank Him that you are now God's child, and confess that from now on He will be the Lord and Love of your life. Give Jesus the key to all the rooms of your heart (Romans 10:9–10; John 1:12).

If I can help your Christian growth in any way, please let me know.

ABOUT THE AUTHOR

Rebecca Barlow Jordan is the author of the popular *Daily in Your Presence: Intimate Conversations with a Loving Father* and *At Home in My Heart: Preparing a Place for His Presence.* She also coauthored the best-selling *Courage for the Chicken Hearted* book series, along with numerous other books. A well-known greeting card writer for over twenty-five years, Rebecca has also penned over sixteen hundred inspirational pieces for magazines, greeting cards, and gift products.

With warmth and transparency, Rebecca loves to share beautiful reflections from the Father's heart at women's conferences, churches, and retreats. She lives in Greenville, Texas, with her husband, Larry—an associate pastor. She has been a Bible study teacher for many years, and as trained marriage enrichment leaders, she and her husband enjoy facilitating marriage enrichment retreats throughout the South. Rebecca's family includes two married daughters and two grandchildren. Her passions include reading, gardening, spending time with family, and learning about the Father's heart.

If this book has encouraged you in any way, Rebecca would love to hear from you. She is also available for speaking engagements by contacting:

Speak Up Speaker Services
Toll free at (888) 870-7719
or at the following E-mail address:
Speakupinc@aol.com

For more information, see Rebecca's Web site at:
www.rebeccabarlowjordan.com

Subject Index